W.H. Strobridge

Catalogue of ancient and modern coins

being the entire collection of Joseph E. Gay

W.H. Strobridge

Catalogue of ancient and modern coins
being the entire collection of Joseph E. Gay

ISBN/EAN: 9783741139635

Manufactured in Europe, USA, Canada, Australia, Japa

Cover: Foto ©ninafisch / pixelio.de

Manufactured and distributed by brebook publishing software (www.brebook.com)

W.H. Strobridge

Catalogue of ancient and modern coins

CATALOGUE

OF

ANCIENT AND MODERN COINS; GEMS; EGYPTIAN ANTIQUITIES; INDIAN IMPLEMENTS, AND RELICS FROM WESTERN MOUNDS; BRIC-A-BRAC; MINERALS, ETC., ETC.

BEING THE ENTIRE COLLECTION OF

JOSEPH E. GAY, Esq.,

OF NEW YORK,

WITH SEVERAL OTHERS OF LESS EXTENT, BESIDES

CONTRIBUTIONS FROM A NUMBER OF GENTLEMEN WHOSE COLLECTIONS IN CERTAIN DEPARTMENTS HAVE BECOME INCONVENIENTLY LARGE.

THE WHOLE TO BE SOLD BY AUCTION

AT

CLINTON HALL,

Astor Place and Eighth Street, New York,

BY

Messrs. GEO. A. LEAVITT & CO., Auctioneers,

On the Afternoons of Wednesday, Thursday, Friday, and Saturday,

April 28th, and following Days.

COMMENCING EACH DAY PUNCTUALLY AT TWO O'CLOCK.

CATALOGUE BY WILLIAM H. STROBRIDGE.

April, 1875.

INTRODUCTION.

It is hardly necessary to say that this is a Catalogue of more than a single collection.

As one, whatever credit it might deserve on the ground of variety, it would lose on that of incongruity; but this is an objection without much force against a catalogue of miscellaneous articles offered for public sale.

That there are several owners in the case, may explain why the catalogue is divided into so many parts and addendas; also why coins of the same class are not sold under one head.

Part I. is composed wholly and exclusively of the collection of Mr. Joseph E. Gay, of New York; and the other gentlemen interested in the sale, will, I am sure, cordially concede that it richly deserves the distinction of being placed at the head. Among the Scotch and English pieces in this collection, are some that will hardly be looked for in a catalogue so unexpected as this will be, and from a cabinet so quietly formed and little known.

In the addendum to Part I., and in Part II. of the Catalogue, many fine coins and medals, both American and foreign, will be found, and collectors will do well to examine this department of the Catalogue with care.

Part III. consists almost wholly of ancient and modern gems, antiquities from Egypt, Bric-a-Brac, and minerals. There are also many good coins in this division, as well as in the addenda to Part II. This will be the last, and by no means the least interesting and important day of the sale. Among the gems are several fine stones; the minerals came from a good collection, and are fit to go into good collections again; the antiquities from Egypt are authentic and valuable. I do not know that we are at liberty to state publicly the facts respecting them, but the writer can do so with propriety in a private way, and besides, exhibit other objects of great value and quite unique, from the same source.

WILLIAM H. STROBRIDGE.

CLINTON HALL, *April* 15, 1875.

INDEX.

PART I.

	PAGE
Early English Coins,	1
Anglo-Norman,	2
English to the Union,	5
Coins of Scotland before the Union,	7
English, from the Union to Victoria,	10
English Silver Medals,	16
Miscellaneous Silver Coins and Medals,	17
Miscellaneous Bronze Medals,	20
American Coins and Medals in Silver,	21
Same in Copper,	22
Same, Political and Miscellaneous,	23
English Copper Coins and Tokens, including English Provincial,	25
Antique, Greek Autonomous, Silver,	27
Same, Regal,	29
Antique Persian, Silver,	30
Antique Greek, Copper,	31
Roman Consular, Silver,	31
Roman Imperial Coins,	33

ADDENDA TO PART I.

Copper Coins, Tokens and Cards,	45
Silver Coins,	46
American Silver,	47
Ancient Silver,	49
Ancient Copper,	50
Modern Silver,	50
Modern Copper,	51

PART II.

American Colonial,	52
Cents,	54
Half Cents,	55
Proof Sets,	56

	PAGE
Pattern Pieces,	56
Gold Coins,	57
Silver Dollars,	57
Half Dollars, Dimes and Half Dimes,	58
Personal and Political Medalets,	59
American Medals,	62
Coins of Mexico,	63
Spanish–Mexican Coins,	65
Central America and Bolivia,	65
La Plata, Peru, and Brazil,	66
West India, and Africa,	67
Coins of England, Silver,	67
Maundy Money and Copper Coins,	68
Coins of France, Silver,	69
Same, Copper,	70
Coins of Spain, Silver,	70
Same, Copper,	71
Coins of Russia,	71
Silver Coins of Austria,	72
Miscellaneous Silver Coins and Medals,	73
Same, Copper,	76
Antique Coins,	78

ADDENDA TO PART II.

English Coins,	78
Miscellaneous Silver, arranged by date,	80
United States Silver,	82
Colonials and Cents,	83
Carrara Medals, and Miscellaneous Medals and Coins,	84
Selected Medals and Coins,	86
Miscellaneous Coins, Medals and Tokens,	87
Fine Silver Coins and Medals,	88

PART III.

Egyptian Bronzes (from Thebes),	89
Antiques in Baked Earth, Glass, Leather, etc.,	90
Engraved Gems,	92
Bric-a-Brac,	95
Indian Implements,	97
Minerals,	97
Collection of Coins, sold as one lot,	100
Book of Postage Stamps,	100
Coin Cabinet,	100

CATALOGUE.

PART I.

EARLY ENGLISH.

1 TOGODUMUS, King in Britain 100 years B. C.; gold stater; fine and rare.
   See Humphrey's Coinage of the British Empire. Pl. 17, No. 4.

2 DRACHMA, horse, under him a wheel, VOL; rev. ear of barley; very fine and rare; silver.

3 HEMI-DRACHM, same type without ins.; fine and rare.

4 COPPER Coin, rude head of Apollo, hair in rolls; rev. horse equally rude (Humphrey, etc., Pl. I, No. 4). Size 14

5 TIN, bull's head front; rev. bear; same period as last; well preserved and very rare.

6 SKEATTÆ of the Heptarchy, rude attempt at a head within a ring of anulets; rev. rude figure (bird ?) and letters; silver; rare.

7 —— Rude head; rev. within a dotted square an anulet (ring) with a dot in centre (H., Pl. II, No. 4); very fine and rare.

8 —— Others, thin silver coin.   2 pieces.

9 STYCAE of Eanred, King of Northumberland A.D. 808.

10 —— of Ethelred   do   do   A.D. 840 (small copper).

11 PENNY of Coenwulf, King of Mercia A.D. 796; diademed head, front face; rev. AMENITA S DEI; fine and extremely rare.

12 —— of Burgred (Mercia), A.D. 852, BVRGRED REX; rev. in three lines, MON + DVDDA, ETA; large size, showing a great improvement in style and execution; as fine as when struck, and very rare.

13 PENNY of Eadmund, King of the East Angles, 885, head crowned; rev. long cross; base.
14 —— of St. Edmund (same time); obv. A, in a circle of dots, SCEAMVN REX; rev. short cross, CREALT MONI; very fine and rare. (Humphrey, Pl. III., 25.)
15 —— of Athelstan, 924–940; EDELSTAN REX TO BRIT; rev. short cross, REGNALD MO EBORIVC (York); broad and fine; very rare.
16 —— Ethelred II., 978; head in profile to left, EDELRED REX; rev. short cross, CHAM O LEERVIC; fine and rare.
17 —— Canute, A.D. 1016, head in profile, CNVT REX ANGLORVM; rev. long cross and tressure, LEFFEL MO NOR; as it came from the die; rare.
18 —— Edward the Confessor, 1040–1042 (he was son of Ethlred); obv. helmeted head in profile to l. and sceptre, EDPADE REX; rev. double cross, square in centre, pellets in the angles; extremely fine and rare.
19 —— Another equally desirable penny of the Confessor, same type; slightly different.
20 —— Harold II., 1066, crowned head in profile and sceptre; rev. across the coin PAX; (see Humphrey, Pl. III., No. 25); extremely fine and rare.

Harold was cotemporary with William of Normandy, "The Conqueror," consequently his coins close the Anglo-Saxon series.

ANGLO-NORMAN.

21 WILLIAM I., 1066–1087; full face penny with crown and sceptre; rev. PAXS in the angles of a cross; as it came from the die; rare.
22 —— Another, same type; equally fine.
23 WILLIAM II. (Rufus), 1087–1100; full face penny, on each side of head a *; rev. voided cross, and quartering it two sceptres crossed; rare type and extremely fine.

This particular penny long ago cost £1 5s.; it was from the collection of Mr. Turnbul, of Philadelphia.

24 HENRY I., 1100–1135; misstruck penny, still fine; rude head in profile, inscription; rev. ornate cross and lilies; very rare.
    Probably struck in Aquitaine.

25 —— Another Penny of Henry I.; head crowned, ¾ face; rev. cross, in each angle a short cross with crosslets; only fair specimen, but it cost 10s. sterling; (from the collection already referred to).

26 HENRY II., 1154–1189; full face, head fleuric and sceptre; rev. short double cross, crosses in angles; brilliant.

27 —— Duplicate, equally fine.

28 RICHARD I., 1189–1199, as Duke of Aquitaine, with his title as King of England, RICHARDVS REX; rev. PIC TAVIE NSIS; uncommonly fine and very rare penny.

29 JOHN, 1199–1216; head in a triangle, IOHANNES REX; rev. crescent and stars in a triangle, ROBERT ON DIVAE; very fine and rare penny.

> James Simon and Henry Noel Humphreys both give us an account of the triangle on this coin, but they do not agree. Simon says he finds heads similarly inclosed on the coins of Biorno, King of Sweden, A.D. 818, and on several of the Kings of France from 893 to 1322; he mentions as examples, coins of Charles the Simple, Philip the Fair, and Charles the Fair; therefore, he concludes that as the King's head was inclosed in a *circle* on English money, for distinction he would be represented in a *triangle* on his Irish coins, particularly as they were now for the first time of the same weight and standard. Simon believes that the harp, which at a later period became the chief symbol of Ireland, was suggested by and proceeded from the triangle, as it was unknown on any coin of that or a former period, now extant.
>
> Mr. Humphreys says without hesitation, "The triangle found on these coins is supposed to be a symbol of the Trinity—the ancient arms of Trinity Priory in Ipswich being represented in a similar manner." The triangle was continued on the Irish coins of Henry III. and Edward I., II., and III., when it disappears.

30 —— Half-penny, full face in a circle, JOHANNES DO +; rev. short cross, an anulet in each quarter; struck in England; extra fine and rare.
  See note in the Groux Catalogue following No. 140.

Anglo-Norman.

31 HENRY III., 1216–1272; obv. same as Henry II.; rev. long double cross; fine penny.
32 —— Half-penny, same type; rare.
33 —— Irish penny; head in a triangle, HENRICVS REX. III.; rev. long cross, three pellets in each quarter; struck at Dublin; fine and rare.
34 EDWARD I., 1273–1307; Penny (known positively), the legend, EDWR ANGL DNS. HYB.; rev. long cross; fair.
35 —— Irish penny, head in a triangle; rev. long cross and pellets; CIVITAS DVBLINIE; extremely fine; rare type.
36 —— Same; struck at Waterford; very rare.
37 EDWARD II., 1307–1327; fine broad penny, EDWAR-RANG DNS. HYB.; struck at Canterbury; scarce.
38 —— Same; struck at London; scarce.
39 EDWARD III., 1327–1377; London penny; good.
40 —— Groat; struck at London; extra fine.
41 EDWARD, The Black Prince, son of Edward III.; Penny of Aquitaine; Lion or Leopard, ŒDVVARDIVS; rev. cross; very rare.

Not verified and possibly erroneous.

42 RICHARD II., 1377–1399; Groat; struck at London; very rare, fine.
43 —— Penny; good and very rare.
44 HENRY IV., 1399–1413; Penny; struck at London; fine.
45 —— Gold Noble; the king in a ship; rev., a cross fleurie and lions crowned; HIS AVTEM TRANSIENS P MEDIVM ILLORVM IBAT; a very beautiful uncirculated coin; very rare.

Celebrated in its day as the finest gold coin in Europe.

46 —— Quarter Noble; very fine and equally rare.
47 HENRY V., 1413–1422; penny; very fine.
48 —— Duplicates; equally fine.   2 pieces
49 —— Groat; VILLA CALISIE; struck at Calais; fine and rare.
50 —— Double Groat; good example; rare.
51 —— Groat; struck at London; very fine.

English Sovereigns to the Union. 5

52 HENRY VI., 1422–1461; Calais Groat; extremely fine.
53 —— Uncirculated ~~Double~~-Groat; rare.
54 —— Groat and Half-Groat. 2 pieces
55 —— Calais Half-Groat; fine. 2 piece
56 EDWARD IV., 1461–1483; Lincoln penny; extremely fine and rare.
57 —— London Groat; extra fine.
58 —— Duplicate; equally fine.
59 —— Groat and Pennies. 3 pieces
60 —— Irish Groat; struck at Waterford; light, but of fine silver; extra fine and rare.

ENGLISH SOVEREIGNS TO THE UNION.

61 HENRY VII., 1483–1509; Groat; struck at London; the crown for the first time arched; uncirculated and beautiful example; rare.
62 —— Duplicate; very fine.
63 —— New coinage; head in profile; rev. shield quartered by a cross, M. M. 2 keys under the shield, which appears for the first time on an English coin; extra fine and rare half-groat.
64 —— Groat, struck for Ireland; obv. arms of England; rev. arms of Ireland, three crowns (see Humphrey, page 96); good, very rare.
65 HENRY VIII., 1509–1547; Groat and Half-Groat. 2 pieces
66 —— Half-Groats; variety. 2 pieces
67 —— Third coinage; head, three-quarter face; rev. arms quartered by a cross; groat, half-groat, and penny; very rare. 3 pieces
68 —— Fifth coinage; head, full face; rev. full-blown rose; base; very rare shilling, rubbed.
69 —— Irish Groat; obv. arms of England; rev. harp and J crowned, A crowned, and K crowned (for several of his wives); good set of 3 pieces.
70 —— English base Groat.

6   *English Sovereigns to the Union.*

71   EDWARD VI., 1547–1553; Testoon (shilling); bust crowned, three-quarter face; to r. XII., to l. rose; rev. coat-of-arms quartered by a cross; very fine, scarce.

72   —— Same; fine, field burnished.

73   —— Shilling and half Shilling.   2 pieces

74   —— Crown, 1551; obv. the King on horseback; rev. coat-of-arms, M. M. ton; coined in the Tower.

  A good example of a rare crown, which, besides being the earliest struck in England, is the first English coin with a date.

75   MARY and Mary and Philip, 1552–1558; Groat of Mary alone; young bust crowned; rev. coat-of-arms; fine and very rare.

76   —— Duplicate; poor.

77   —— Shilling of Mary and Philip, their busts vis-a-vis; above, crown; rev. arms on oval shield; above, XII. and crown; in very good condition and rare.

78   —— Base Irish Shilling of same; below bust date (1555); rev. harp; not much circulated, scarce.

79   ELIZABETH, 1558–1602; Shilling, Sixpence, Threepence, Twopence, and Three-farthings; very fine set of her hammered money.   5 pieces

80   —— Milled Shilling; the edge grained, the inner circle taken away; very fine and rare.

81   —— Milled Sixpence; extremely fine, rare.

82   —— Shilling, Sixpence, and Threepence; hammered coins; fine.   3 pieces

83   —— Six-pence and Threepence; same.   2 pieces

84   —— Six-pences and Twopence pierced.   4 pieces

85   —— Crown; bust crowned, with orb and sceptre (this is the first time the sceptre appears since Henry III.), legend, POSVI DEVM ADIVTOREM MEVM; very fine, highly desirable and valuable.

86   —— Gold Angel (23½ carat fine); arms on a ship; rev. St. Michael and Dragon; a fine coin, only bent, could be easily straightened; very rare.   Size 20

87   —— Irish Shilling of fine silver; rev. 3 harps on shield crowned; rare.

88   —— Irish Groats with and without bust; base.   3 pieces

COINS OF SCOTLAND BEFORE THE UNION.

89 WILLIAM I., 1165–1214; Penny; side face and sceptre; rev. cross with crescents in the angles; extremely fine, and undoubtedly a coin of William the Lion; extremely rare.

90 ALEXANDER II., A.D. 1214; fine Penny; crowned head to l., before face, sceptre; rev. double cross, in each angle a star; rare.

91 ALEXANDER III., A.D. 1249; similar obv.; on rev. long cross, etc.; very fine.

92 —— Half-penny; same type; very rare.

93 JOHN (BALIOL), A.D. 1292–1306; Penny; also half-faced with crown and sceptre; JOHANNES DEI GRA; rev. REX SCOTORVM, cross with the stars as before; fine and extremely rare.

94 DAVID II., 1329–1371; Penny; executed exactly in the style of his predecessors; DAVID REX, etc.; uncirculated, rare.

95 —— Half-groat; crowned and side-faced head of the King with sceptre erect, DAVID DEI GRATIA REX SCOTORVM; rev. DNS PROTECTOR, MS., & LIBERATOR MS on outer circle, and VILLA EDINBVRGH on an inner, all divided by a cross; extremely fine and rare.

96 —— Groat; exactly the same and apparently uncirculated; rare.

<small>He was the first in Scotland who coined groats and half-groats.</small>

97 ROBERT II., 1371–1390; groat like that of David II., except ROBERTVS, etc.; fine, rare.

98 ROBERT III., 1390–1406; groat; the King's head, full face and crown without the sceptre. [The tressure around the head on this, as also on English groats of the period, was designed to represent a rose.] Rev. three globules in each quarter of a cross; beautiful and rare.

99 JAMES I., 1406–1437; light groat (1 dr. 9 grs.); bust full face, with crown and sceptre; rev. in the quarters of a

cross, two fleurs de lis and twice three little balls, an inner circle bearing VILLA EDINBVRGH, and on outer DNS PROTECTOR MS, etc.; in good preservation, and very rare.

100 JAMES II., 1437-1460; groat (ordered by act of Parliament to pass for 14 pennies;) his head, full face and crown without sceptre; rev. crowns and balls in the angles of a cross; weight 2 dr. 8 grs.; fine and very rare.

101 —— Another, largely debased; very rare.

102 JAMES III., 1460-1488; billon coin called at the time, "Black penny," now rare.

> It was in this reign that Parliament ordained that, "For the ease and sustentation of the King's Lieges and almous deede to be done to puir folk, there be cunzied copper money, four to the penny, havand on the ane part, the croce of S. Andrew and th' crown on th' other part, with subscription of EDINBVRGH on the ane part, and ane R with James on the other part." These are the same pieces that in the reign of James VI. got the name of "Atchesons," from a coiner of money by that name.

103 JAMES IV., 1488-1513; Black Penny.

104 —— Groat of fine silver; open face with crown; JACOBVS DEV GRA REX SCOTORVM; rev. hexagonal mullets and three balls, repeated in the angles of the cross; inner and outer circle with inscriptions; extremely rare, fine.

105 JAMES V., 1513-1542; billon plack and half plack; on one side a thistle, on the other, St. Andrew's cross; very fine. 2 pieces

106 MARY, 1542-1587; billon plack; uncirculated, rare.

107 —— New billon coin; lion on the Scotch shield; rev. cross open in the centre with a small cross therein, crown in the angles; uncirculated.

108 —— Testoon of the exact value of the English shilling, its current value 5 shillings *Scotch*, 1558; obv. the Scotch shield supported by the letters M and R; MARIA DEI G SCOTOR REGINA; rev. large cross, with a small cross in each quarter; TN VIRTVTE TVA LIBERA MEA; strictly uncirculated, rare.

109 —— Silver crown of an ounce weight; obv. the shield of Scotland crowned and supported by two thistles;

MARIA DEI GRA SCOTORVM REGINA ; rev. a Palm tree crowned ; the motto "Dat Gloria vires," hanging on it ; 15–67 (after her second husband's death) ; the legend circumscribed upon this beautiful coin is EXVRGAT DEVS DISSIPENTR INIMICI EJVS ; uncirculated, ex. rare.

<blockquote>William Nicholson, Arch-Deacon of Carlisle, in his "Scottish Historical Library," published in 1702, in the course of a short account of the medals and coins of Scotland, makes the following observation: "Some call the tree on the reverse, an *Yew Tree*, and report that there grew a famous one of that kind in the Park (or Garden) of the Earl of *Lenox*, which gave occasion to the impress."</blockquote>

110 MARY, with Henry Darnley ; their coin of two-thirds of an ounce of the same type, the title being MARIA & HENRIC, etc. ; a thistle counterstamped on rev. ; 1586 ; very fine and rare.

<blockquote>This piece went for twenty shillings *Scotch*, the large one going for thirty shillings ; there were also 10 and 5 shilling pieces with the same impression.</blockquote>

111 —— Gold Lion ; obv. Scotch shield crowned, J-G supporting ; MARIA DEI GRA R SCOTORVMT ; rev. cypher of her name crowned, DILIGITE IVSTICIAM 1553 ; uncirculated, brilliant, extra rare. [Now valued at £5.]

112 JAMES VI., 1587–1625 ; XXX piece of an ounce weight ; obv. shield of Scotland crowned, supported by the letters J R, both crowned ; rev. a sword upright with a crown on its point, date 1570 ; legend " Pro me Si mereor in me ; " very fine and rare crown.

<blockquote>Nicholson says, " This motto was borrowed from Trajan, whose saying it was on the delivery of the Praetors sword; George Buchanan was James' tutor and probably suggested it."</blockquote>

113 —— Mark, 1573 ; obv. Scottish shield crowned ; rev. cross with thistles and crowns in alternate quarters ; SALVA FAC POPVLVM TVVM DNC ; in excellent preservation, and very rare.

114 —— XXX shilling piece of ⅔ oz. weight ; obv. the young King crowned, holding a sword upright ; rev.

arms crowned HONOR REGIS JVDICIVM DILICIT, 1582; extremely fine and rare.

Of these it appears there were coined pieces of 20, 10 and 5 shillings, as well the one here given.

115 JAMES VI., balance mark of 1591; Scotch arms crowned; rev. naked sword and balance, HIS DIFFERS REGE TYRANNVS; weight, 2 dwt. 14 grs; in good preservation, and rare.

116 —— Mark, with the portraiture of his Majesty's body on obverse; rev. a thistle, NEMO ME IMPVNE LACESSET, 1594; fine and very rare.

117 —— Thistle mark, half mark, quarter and eighth do. 1602; these have the Royal shield of Scotland crowned; rev. same as last, hence the name, thistle mark; a very good set (one pierced), of four rare pieces.

118 —— Gold thistle crown without date (but after the Union); on one side the rose of England crowned, on the other, the thistle of Scotland crowned; the titles round the rose, with motto on rev. "Tueatur Unita Deus;" extremely fine and rare.

119 JAMES VIII. (the Pretender), 1716; obv. laureated bust, JACOBVS VIII DEI GRATIA; rev. arms on four shields as a cross, with the cross of St. Andrew thereon; REX SCO AN FRA ET HIB; a beautiful uncirculated pattern coin, or perhaps medal of the greatest rarity. Size 20

ENGLISH SOVEREIGNS FROM JAMES I. TO VICTORIA.

120 JAMES I., 1602–1625; Shillings, different dies; good. 2 pieces

121 —— Sixpence; rev. English coat-of-arms; fine.

122 —— Same; rev. harp (Irish); very fine, rare.

123 —— Twopence, penny, and half-penny, one pierced, otherwise very desirable; rare. 3 pieces

124 —— Twopence; rose crowned and thistle crowned; fine.

125 —— Same, and penny with bust; very good, rare. 2 pieces

126 —— Twopence and penny; very good. 2 pieces

English Sovereigns from James I. to Victoria.

127 JAMES I., Gold unit, called also "broad piece;" obv. the King to r., crowned with orb and sceptre; rev. arms crowned, J—R; but little circulated, but pierced; rare.
Size 24

128 —— Gold double-crown of 10 shillings; obv. laureated bust to left; rev. arms, and the legend, HENRICVS ROSAS REGNA JACOBVS; uncirculated, very rare.

129 CHARLES I., 1625–1649; set of coins answering to the "maunday money," struck regularly in succeeding reigns; viz.: 4d., 3d., 2d., and 1d.; fine, one slightly pierced, very rare. 4 pieces

130 —— Sixpence; rev. in three straight lines, REL PROT LEG ANG LIB PAR, 1646; extremely fine for type, rare.

131 —— Milled shilling; nearly uncirculated, very rare.

132 —— Shilling and sixpence, milled; rare, but ordinary. 2 pieces

133 —— Shilling, without inner circle, the arms on round shield; fine and rare.

134 —— Shilling, twopence, and rose penny. 3 pieces

135 —— Ormond groat (obsidional); C. R. under a crown; rev. IIII.; rare.

136 —— Newark shilling (also obsidional); lozenge shape; pierced, but fine and rare.

137 —— Half-crown; the King on horseback; rev. coat-of-arms on round shield; not well struck, but sharp; a desirable piece, rare.

138 —— Crown, same type; M. M. Bell; broad and well-preserved, though considerably circulated.

139 —— For Scotland; bust crowned; rev. thistle crowned, XL (pence); size of English sixpence, good example.

140 —— Same, XX (pence); fine.

141 —— Same, XL and XX; good. 2 pieces

142 COMMONWEALTH, 1648–1660; beautiful and perfect set, from shilling to half-penny, dated 1652: XII, VI, II, I, and ½d.; very fine and rare. 5 pieces

143 —— Duplicate penny; pierced.

144 —— Gold sovereign or XX-shilling piece, dated 1649; pierced and slightly bent, but rare and desirable.

12 *English Sovereigns from James I. to Victoria.*

145 CROMWELL to 1660; shilling; gilt, very good, rare.

146 —— Half-crown, 1658; laureated bust; rev. coat-of-arms crowned; his escutcheon on the arms of England, Scotland, and Ireland; motto, PAX QVÆRITVR BELLO; BRILLIANT PROOF, extremely rare.

147 —— Crown, same type; fine proof, equally rare.

148 CHARLES II., 1660–1684; 4d., 3d., 2d., and penny, from Simon's dies (crowned bust); not uncirculated, very good. 4 pieces

149 —— 4d., 3d., 2d., and penny; his cypher crowned, with laureated bust; all fine. 4 pieces

150 —— Sixpence; laureated bust to r.; rev. arms on four shields arranged as a cross, in each angle two C's interlaced; very fine.

151 —— Shilling, same type; equally fine.

152 —— Half-crown, same; very fine.

153 —— Crown, same type, 1663; very fine.

154 —— Crown, a variety of this type dated 1673; very fine.

A superb series, and probably never in circulation.

155 —— Half-crown for Scotland; arms on four shields as before, with the interlacing C's, but, on this, the place of France is filled by the arms of Scotland, repeated; in the centre, XX^{VI}; rubbed, but very rare.

156 —— Shilling and sixpence of the same type; in the centre of cross XII and VI; very fine, rare. 2 pieces

157 —— Shilling; head reversed, and in the angles of the cross a thistle; also the half-shilling; in fair preservation. 2 pieces

158 —— Bawbees and other coppers; some of Charles I., and perhaps other reigns not examined, but all with the Scotch arms; good lot. 16 pieces

159 JAMES II., 1684–1688; 4d., 3d., and 2d. of the Maunday set; rubbed. 3 pieces

160 —— Shilling, 1685; uncirculated and brilliant, very rare.

161 —— Crown, 1688; uncirculated, although the laurel wreath shows marks of the drawer—the reverse, none whatever; a splendid crown, rare.

English Sovereigns from James I. to Victoria.

162 JAMES II., Gold coin, without date; obv. a ship under full sail; rev. St. Michael in combat with the dragon, SOLI DEO GLORIA; pierced, about ½ guinea, and, I should think, rare.

163 —— Scotch shilling (10 under bust); poor.

164 —— Same, 40-shilling piece; extremely fine, about ⅞ of an ounce weight, or nearly the size of the English crown; in this fine condition, very rare.

165 WILLIAM and Mary and William III., 1688–1702; Maunday money of W. and M.; two of the pieces uncirculated.   4 pieces

166 —— 4d. and 2d. of same; very fine.   2 "

167 —— Sixpence; in the quarters of the cross cypher of their names; ex. fine.

168 —— Shilling of same type; equally fine.

169 —— Half-crown; rev. coat-of-arms on plain shield crowned; good.

170 —— Scotch crown; 60-schilling *Scotch*, 1692; good, but circulated, rare.

171 —— Same, 10-shillings, Scotch; fine.

172 —— Shilling and Sixpence of William alone 1696; very fine.   2 pieces

173 —— Scotch 40-Shilling piece of William alone 1698; nearly uncirculated, rare.

174 —— Same, 10 and 5-Shilling, *Scotch;* very good.   2 pieces

175 ANNE, 1702–1714; Maundy Money; full set, very fine.   4 pieces

176 —— Sixpence, 1703; under the bust, VIGO; extremely fine.

177 —— Shilling and Sixpence, 1711; equally fine.   2 pieces

178 —— Duplicate Shilling of this date; very fine.

179 —— Five and Ten Shillings, *Scotch*.   2 pieces

180 —— The same, repeated.   2 pieces

181 —— Half Crown E(dinburgh), under bust; good.

182 GEORGE I., 1714–1727; Maundy Money; a full set; uncirculated, rare.   4 pieces

14 *English Sovereigns from James I. to Victoria.*

183 GEORGE I., Shilling of the South Sea Co.'s Silver; uncirculated, rare.
184 —— Shilling, with roses and feathers in the angles of the cross; very fine.
185 —— Half Crown, S. S. C.; rare type, but pierced.
186 GEORGE II., 1729–1760; Maundy Money; 3d., 2d., and 1d.; uncirculated, rare. 3 pieces
187 —— Sixpences; young head, roses and feathers; old head, plain; and same with LIMA under bust; uncirculated. 3 pieces
188 —— Shilling, old head; uncirculated, rare.
189 —— Same, very fine.
190 —— Half Crown, roses and plume; young head; circulated.
191 —— Crown, young head; in each angle of the cross a rose, 1739; *extremely fine*, rare.
192 —— Same, with roses and *plumes;* equally fine and rare.
193 —— Gold Coins struck for Hanover, 1754 and 1756; ¼ GOLD G., ½ THAL.; two varieties, uncirculated and brilliant; rare. 2 pieces
194 GEORGE III., 1760–1820; Maundy Money; full set, with young head; uncirculated. 4 pieces
195 —— Another set, different; young head; about 1800; also uncirculated. 4 pieces
196 —— Maundy Money, 3d., 2d., and 1d. 3 "
197 —— Same, old and young heads; uncirculated; some proof; 3 4d's and 3 pennies. 6 pieces
198 —— Shilling, 1787; brilliant.
199 —— Half Crown, 1816; arms on round shield, surround by chain of the Order of St. George and the Garter; uncirculated.
200 —— Shilling, same date; fine.
201 —— Sixpence, do brilliant.
202 —— Bank Token, do 1s. 6d.; uncirculated.
203 —— do 10d. Irish and English 6d. 2 pieces
204 —— Dollar of Bank of England, 1804; has been circulated.

GEORGE III., Crown of 1818, from Pistrucci's dies; extremely fine uncirculated coin, rare.
—— Brilliant untarnished proof from these dies; has been preserved in this condition in a box padded with cotton; valued in London at £2.
—— Gold ½ Guinea; uncirculated.
—— do ⅓ do   2 varieties.   2 pieces
—— do ¼ do
GEORGE IV., 1820–1830; Maundy Money; full set, proof. 4 pieces
—— Shilling and Sixpence, 1824; laureated bust; rev. arms within the garter; uncirculated, scarce. 2 pieces
—— Shilling and Sixpence, 1825; bare bust (Chantrey's); rev. crown and lion; uncirculated, scarce. 2 pieces
—— Sixpence of both types; uncirculated. 2 pieces
—— Half Crown, 1825; rev. "Britanniarum Rex," etc.; very good.
—— Crown from Pistrucci's dies, laureated bust; rev. St. George and Dragon; circulated.
—— Proof Crown from new dies, lettered edge; obv. bare bust, 1826; rev. garnished shield crowned; on a schedule "Dieu et mon Droit," circumscribed by legend BRITANNIORUM REX; engraved by Wyon from Chantrey's bust; very rare.
WILLIAM IV. 1830–1837; Maundy Money; full set, fine proof. 4 pieces
—— Half Crown, 1834; fine.
VICTORIA, 1837 to date; Maundy Money; full set, proof. 4 pieces
—— Another set, also fine proofs. 4 "
—— Canada 25, 10, and 5 cents; uncirculated. 3 "
—— Shilling, sixpence, fourpence, and penny-halfpenny; uncirculated. 4 pieces
—— Sixpence, fourpence, and penny-half-penny; uncirculated. 3 pieces
—— Florin, "1/10 of a pound," 1849; an omission in the legend; uncirculated, rare.
—— The same, with and without "Dei Gratiæ," in legend; uncirculated, rare. 2 pieces

16   *English Silver Medals.*

226 VICTORIA, series of her coins from crown to penny, with the exception of the first, uncirculated; as a set, rare.

8 pieces

ENGLISH SILVER MEDALS.

227 JAMES I. and Charles I.; engraved medal, with busts of both—" Give thy judgments, O God, unto the king, and thy righteousness unto the king's sonne;" much bent and abused.   Size 16

228 CHARLES I., Coronation Medal, Feb. 2, 1626; young bust, royally dressed, collar and crown; rev. mailed arm issuing from a cloud, in the hand a sword DONEC PAX REDDITA TERRIS; on both sides a beaded circle; made by the mill and screw process; fine, and in fine preservation.   Size 18

229 CHARLES II., Coronation, Medal April 23, 1861; bust crowned, with collar and chain of the Order of St. George, under the arm T. S. (Thomas Simon); rev. an angel crowning a king; very fine and rare.   Size 18

230 WILLIAM and MARY, their busts as they are represented on coins; rev. a sea monster approaching a rocky shore, where a man stands chained to a cliff; St. George descending to his rescue; 1689; very fine and rare.   Size 24

231 WILLIAM III., " The glorious and immortal memory, 1690," William of Orange on horseback; rev. " King and Country;" arms surmounted by crown and lion, the supporters standing on the schedule with national motto, by *Mossop;* pierced, but very fine, nearly proof, and very rare.   Size 28

232 ANNE, 1702; on her inauguration; bust in Roman style; rev. Minerva attacking a monster with three heads. VICEM GERIT ILLA TONANTIS. Extremely fine, nearly proof.   Size 22

233 —— 1704; on a naval victory off Gibraltar; view of the action; in foreground three shields suspended from a palm tree; at its foot, Britannia, as acknowledged mistress of the seas; ex. fine.   Size 26

Miscellaneous Silver Coins and Medals.

234 ANNE, 1707; medalet; obv. bust, royally draped; order chain St. George and crown; rev. shield on a pedestal, the supporters lying down; extremely fine. Size 16

235 —— 1708; bust; rev. two captives bound at the foot of a triumphal column; fine medal but much rubbed on reverse; by T. C. Size 30

236 —— 1713, by same; bust, rev. Minerva standing with a handful of flowers; ordinary. Size 22

237 GEORGE I., 1714; on his coronation; fine medal, by same hand. Size 22

238 GEORGE IV., 1815, as Prince Regent; "Wellington, Waterloo." Medal by *T. Wyon;* one of the best that I have seen.

239 —— On his death, July 15, 1830; obv. his bust, after Chantrey; rev. urn and symbolical representation of the loss sustained in his death by the nation and by several of the liberal arts. Beautiful medal by *Sorgram;* proof, with a few scratches; rare. Size 3

240 VICTORIA, 1849; War in India; two bars, GOOGERAT and CHILIANWALA; fine proof, by *Wyon.*

241 —— 1854; War in Crimea, by same; 4 bars, nearly proof.

MISCELLANEOUS SILVER COINS AND MEDALS.

242 ENGLISH Colonial ⅛ and 1/16 crown, and 10 cents Sierra Leone Co. 3 pieces

243 —— Hong Kong dollar; very fine; scarce.

244 —— Same; 20, 10, and 5 cents. 3 pieces

245 —— Ceylon "One Rix Dollar," (Geo. IV.); beautiful proof; very rare.

246 ENGLISH Shilling Tokens. 5 pieces

247 —— Sixpence Tokens and small coins; in the lot several proofs of Maundy sets. 10 pieces

248 —— Brunswick ½ crown of Geo. II; very fine.

249 IRISH Penny of Sithric I., A.D. 989; good and rare.

18   *Miscellaneous Silver Coins and Medals.*

250 BRACTEATE of the old city of Halle, in Germany; early Russian coins; Wild Man coins of Brunswick, etc.; fine and rare lot.   8 pieces

251 RUSSIA, for Poland, 1836; coin of Holland; Spain, of Charles II., Sigismund I., etc.; an extremely choice lot, dime size.   12 pieces

252 ISABEL II.; Spanish 10 Reals (half dollar) 1852; uncirculated; scarce.

253 WILLIAM and AUGUSTA, Prussia; their thaler struck before the war—1861; uncirculated, scarce.

254 MAXIMILLIAN; Mexican Dollar, 1866; extremely fine.; scarce.

255 —— Duplicate, equally fine.

256 JAPAN; new coinage; Quarter Yen; obv. Sun within circle of beads; around this, branches of trees and flowers; rev. dragons circumscribed by oriental characters; edge reeded; brilliant; value 25 cents; rare.

257 —— Same, dime size, $\tfrac{1}{10}$ Yen.

258 TIGURINIAE (Zurich); Half Thaler medal with view of the city; fine.

259 RUSSIAN Rouble Medal of Alexander I., 1834; bust, rev. Monument; fine proof.

260 BRUNSWICK Crown of 1606; coat-of-arms with 5 crests; rev. wild man; very fine broad crown under John Frederick, Grand Duke.   Size 30

261 —— Similar under Anthony Ulrich; uncirculated and brilliant.   Size 30

262 SAXONY; Crown of 1540; John Frederick and Henry; Dukes and brothers, a bust of each; very good and rare.

263 PAPAL of Innocent XII.; beautiful medal crown; obv. bust.; rev. a mole, sail-boats riding secure; VENT ET MARE OBEDIVNT EI MD-CIC; uncirculated, rare.

264 —— of Clement XII., 1732; splendid medal, crown size, but much thicker; bust; rev. JVSTITIA FIRMATVR SOLIVM ANNO SALVTIS, etc.; in exergue, coat-of-arms and symbols; very rare.

Miscellaneous Silver Coins and Medals. 19

265 RELIGIOUS Square Medalet and reliquary; has been worn on a rosary; very old and curious.
266 AUGSBURG Confession Klippe in Memory, etc.; 25 June, 1630, the first centenary; as perfect and bright as when struck; a gem. Size 16 x 14
267 CHARLES I., England, and his Queen; their busts on an oval pendant medalet, worn by a Royalist of the time; about the same size as last.
268 KLIPPE; two Cornucopiæ crossed, a star above, SLAM; rev. the Angel of Time. Size 16 x 16
269 ERIN Badge; within a circle of stars on a heart-shaped shield, a harp and the inscription ERIN; very beautiful; 2½ x 2 inches, with loop.
270 RELIGIOUS Oval Medal; very old.
270* MEDALET of Louis le Grand and companion. Size 8. 2 pieces
271 CORONATION Medalets, German; fine proofs. Size 17. 2 pieces
272 RATISBON Medalet in honor of Francis I.; bust; rev. the city, and companion, equally fine; not known; an extremely fine pair. Size 20. 2 pieces
273 PROCLAMATION Medal of Charles IV. of Spain, 1789; cast half dollar size; fine, and doubtless rare; unknown.
274 ENGRAVED Masonic Medal, dollar size.
275 GERMAN Medals, half dollar size; a storm; rev. a town in ruins, ZEIGT DER RUIN IN BRESLAV; 21 June, 1749; and beautiful love medal, same size; doves cooing, and male and female plighting their vows; fine and valuable. 2 pieces
276 MEDAL, by Looz; one of his beautiful proofs; DOCH MEINE LIEBE NICHT; and Janus medal by same hand, but inferior; thaler size. 2 pieces
277 SWEDISH Klippe Dollar of John III., 1571; J. R. divided by a cross supporting a crown; rev. 3 crowns DEVS PROTECTOR NOSTR (15)71; fine and ex. rare.
278 RELIGIOUS MEDAL; the Athanasian Creed; rev. symbolical; extremely fine, dollar size.

Miscellaneous Bronze Medals.

279 BONAPARTE MEDAL; bust and titles of the "Premier Consul;" rev. figure of Peace PAX DE LVNEVILLE LE XX PLVVIOSE AN IX; thick medal, dollar size, nearly proof; very rare.

280 MARRIAGE MEDAL of Alexander and Caroline, Emperor of Russia and Princess of Brunswick and Luneburg, 1711; it contains about 2 oz. silver; battered.

281 WILLIAM II., Elector, etc., Marburg; fine military bust; rev. 3 civic crowns and ins. XXVIII July, MDCCC-XXVII; about 3 oz. weight, and very fine.

282 SIAM bullet Dollar.

282* —— Duplicate.

283 JAPAN ¼ Itzbu. 2 pieces

283* MISCELLANEOUS Medalets and Coins. 4 pieces

Miscellaneous Gold Coins.

284 MOHUR, India; about 4 Rupees.

285 PAGODA, Persia; same value, or nearly so; fine proof; rare.

286 RUPEE (gold), Assam.

287 BESHLIK, Turkey; fine proof and ½ do.; poor. 2 pieces

288 DUCAT, Francis Lauredano, Doge of Venice; fine and extremely rare.

289 —— of the Belgic Confederacy, 1829; fine.

290 CAROLINA Gold Bechtler Dollar.

291 CALIFORNIA Half-dollars, round and octagon. 3 pieces

292 —— Quarter-dollars, " " " 3 "

293 BYZANTINE old ¼ Aureus, unknown; rare.

MISCELLANEOUS BRONZE MEDALS.

294 ANNE, Queen of England; bust; rev. arms and crown, cupids supporting, each holding one end of the order-chain of St. George; below, rose and thistle; on a schedule, SEMPER EADEM; fine proof, by Crocker.
Size 22

295 NICHOLAS I., Czar of Russia; bust; rev. within oak-wreath, PRAEMIA DIGNO; fine proof. Size 40

American Coins and Medals—Silver. 21

296 COLOGNE CATHEDRAL; Jubilee of the 14th Aug., 1848; view of the edifice finished and unfinished; very fine.
Size 38
297 JOHN FRANCIS DUCIS, "Accord d'un beau talent et de d'un beau caractere," 1816, by *Gatteaux;* fine proof.
Size 24
298 LIBERTY AND EQUALITY; French Medal, Liberty seated; rev. "En 1789, en 1830, le PEUPLE vanqueur de la royante," struck in 1832; fine proof. Size 24
299 MEDAL by *Andrieu,* Fidélité dévouement; rev. star of 5 points, embossed with shield, lily and inscription.
Size 24
300 MOLIERE, Gretry, Corneille; their busts accolated; rev. a harp; splendid medal by *Veyrat.* Size 24
301 MAJ.-GEN. LORD HUTCHINSON; military bust; rev. "Egypt delivered;" splendid medal by *Webb.* Size 24
302 LIEUT.-GEN. LORD LYNEDOCH; rev. ST. SEBASTIAN, Aug. 31, 1813; fine and rare medal by *Mudie.* Size 24
304 CHARLES IV. OF SPAIN; religious oval medal and two others. Av. size 24. 4 pieces

AMERICAN COINS AND MEDALS.
Silver.

305 DOLLAR of 1795; flowing hair; circulated, but fine.
306 —— 1797; before the face, 7 stars.
307 —— 1799; very fine.
308 HALF DOLLAR of 1794; much rubbed, scarce.
309 —— 1795; less rubbed, scarce.
310 —— 1806; uncirculated, scarce.
311 QUARTER DOLLAR, 1796; much circulated, but fair, rare.
312 —— 1805; less circulated.
313 —— Spanish Dollar; cut for convenience, rare.
314 DIME of 1796 and half do, 1795; one pierced; poor, rare.
2 pieces
315 PINE TREE SHILLING; poor, rare.
316 OAK TREE do pierced, but fine, rare.
317 ANAPOLIS do good example, not fine, rare.

22   *American Coins and Medals—Copper.*

318 MARTHA WASHINGTON half dime; much circulated, rare.
319 CAROLINA MEDAL; circulated, but fine.   Size 23
320 INDIAN PEACE MEDAL, by Congress to M. Van Buren, 1837; bust; rev. two clasping hands; hatchet and pipe; ring attached as worn by Indian chief; about 3 ozs.; fine, scarce.
321 OATH OF ALLEGIANCE MEDAL; bust of Washington; rev. inscription; fine proof.   Size 22
322 WASHINGTON MEDALET; bust; rev. born and died; proof.   Size 12
322* —— Rev. Jackson; fine proof.   "
323 MATTHEWS MEDAL, "Soda-water apparatus," 437 1st Av., New York; splendid proof; the only one in silver; in velvet case; mounted to show both sides; dies by Muller.   Size 18

Copper.

324 ROSA-AMERICANA PENNY, 1722 (half-penny *English*); laureated bust of George I.; rev. full-blown rose; very fine.
325 WOOD'S HALF-PENNY (same size); obv. same; rev. Hibernia, 1723; dark, but nearly uncirculated.
326 —— Same; varieties, with the harp both before and behind the figure of Hibernia; in fine and fair condition; one rare.   2 pieces
327 VIRGINIA HALF-PENNY, 1773; uncirculated.
328 —— Same, dark; rather poor.   2 pieces
329 KENTUCKY CENT; no date; very good.
330 NEW YORK, "Nova-Constellatio;" two varieties, 1783.   2 pieces
331 —— Same; repeated.   2   "
332 VERMONT, "Vermon Auctori," 1788; laureated head to right; nearly uncirculated; seldom seen as fine, rare.
333 —— "Vermontensium Res Publicæ; very good, rare.
334 CONNECTICUT, "Auctori Connec.;" uncirculated, but not evenly struck; very desirable, rare.
335 —— Varieties; very fair lot.   3 pieces
336 MASSACHUSETTS, 1788, cent; only fair.
337 —— Half-cent; fine, rare.

Political and Miscellaneous Medals, etc. 23

338 NEW JERSEY and Franklin Cents. 2 pieces
339 TALBOT, ALLUM & LEE, 1794, Cent; nearly uncirculated.
340 WASHINGTON Cent, 1791; rev. large eagle; very good but dark.
341 —— Unity States; very good.
342 UNITED STATES Cent, 1793; flowing hair; rev. wreath; very poor.
343 —— Half Cent, same date; very good, rare.
344 —— Feuchtwanger's Composition, 1837; fine. 2 pieces
345 —— Pattern Nickel Cent of 1856; proof, very rare.
346 —— Uncirculated Cents of 1856 and '7; bright; nickel and copper. 4 pieces
347 —— Restruck "Non-Dependens-Status"; fine proof.
348 LAFAYETTE MEDAL, by *Caunois*, "Defender," etc.; tarnished proof, 1777–1824. Size 32
349 FRANKLIN MEDAL, by *Dupré*, "Eripuis Coele," etc.; fine proof, 1786. Size 32
350 —— With Montyon; their busts accolated; by *Barre*, 1833; tarnished proof. Size 30
351 WEBSTER, by *C. C. Wright*; bare bust; rev. globe on monument; inscribed on base, I STILL LIVE; fine proof. Size 48
352 MAJ. SCOTT, by *Furst*; bust in military habit; rev. resolution of Congress, etc.; 1844; fine proof. Size 40
353 LINCOLN, by *Ellis*, 1862; bust in civilian dress; rev. Indians at work, circumscribed by a representation of Indian life in the savage state; fine proof. Size 48
354 ELECTROTYPE copies of Washington Medals; one, Stony Point fortified; extremely rare. 2 pieces

Political and Miscellaneous Medals and Tokens.

355 MARTIN VAN BUREN; "Sober Second Thought," "Weighed in the Balance," and "Independent Treasury;" copper and brass. 4 pieces
356 WILLIAM HENRY HARRISON; full-face and side-face, log cabin, Tippecanoe, etc.; many varieties, copper and brass. 5 pieces
357 —— Repetition nearly; and "Loco Foco line." 5 pieces

24   *Political and Miscellaneous Medals, etc.*

358 WILLIAM HENRY HARRISON, Military bust; rev. log cabin and flag, tree at each end of house, cider barrel and mug to left, "The people's choice—the hero of Tippecanoe;" tin, fine.   Size 24
359 HENRY CLAY; "United we Stand," and W. H. Seward; fine.   2 pieces
360 JOHN C. FREMONT and GEN. SCOTT; "Jessie's choice;" very fine.   5 pieces
361 FILMORE and PIERCE; brass.   2 pieces
362 ZACH. TAYLOR; bust; rev. ins.; copper, gilt; fine.   Size 20
363 OLD HICKORY, Martin Van Buren and Anthony Wayne, new series; fine proofs, uniform; copper and brass.   3 pieces
364 JOHN BELL, Abraham Lincoln, and Stephen A. Douglas, 1860; copper, brass, and tin; size 18, very fine and bright, not uniform; valuable lot.   8 pieces
365 —— A. Lincoln, 1860; rev., rail-fence; copper, proof.   Size 22
366 JOHN C. BRECKENRIDGE; rev. White House, "Our Country and Our Rights;" plain, and with copper and brass centres, as they were struck; copper, brass, and metal.   6 pieces
367 JAMES BUCHANAN, M. Filmore, and J. C. Fremont, campaign medals; uniform, by *S. & H., N. Y.*; tin. Size 22.   3 pieces
368 "SABBATH-SCHOOL JUBILEE, July 4, 1842," and Bunker Hill Monument; in thick copper; mules, one without reverse.   2 pieces
369 JOHN C. FREMONT, by *S. & H.*; published by Ball, Black & Co.; rev. surveying party; proof, tin.   Size 32
370 CAMPAIGN MEDALS; Lincoln, Douglas, Breckenridge, by *True;* set in lead; really rare. Size 28.   3 pieces
371 —— Douglas and Breckenridge, of same.   2 pieces
372 —— Lincoln, by *Childs;* and Lincoln and Hamlin, with two rails crossed; in nickle and tin.   2 pieces
373 JOHN ADAMS, of Presidential series by *G. H. S.;* bust; rev. residence; fine proof, copper.

374 BENJ. FRANKLIN; rev. "Time is Money," by *Merriam*; fine proof, copper.
375 ROBERT FULTON; rev. Steam Navigation, etc.; brass. Size 24
376 GEORGE H. LOVETT'S CARD; rev. Washington on horseback; fine proof, copper.
377 PIONEER BASE BALL CLUB, and Fireman's Medal; proof, copper and brass. 2 pieces
378 GEO. B. MCCLELLAN; Brimslow's Washington, etc.; in copper, brass, and tin; fine lot. 8 pieces
379 EMANCIPATION MEDAL in tin—Negro in chains and Negro with his fetters broken—copy of Shekel and Temperance Medal; proof, tin. 3 pieces
380 THE ANTIQUARY, 1859; Liberia Cent, "I am Ready," 1861; fine. 3 pieces
381 "MASSACHUSETTS & California Co., 5 D"(ollars); in copper, from the dies for their issue of gold; very fine, rare.
382 MELANOTYPES and Clay Buttons. 10 pieces
383 COPPERHEADS; bright and uncirculated. 186 pieces

ENGLISH COPPER COINS AND TOKENS.

[English Provinces included under this Head.]

384 CHARLES I.; Farthings, varieties; two sceptres crossed through a crown, on some a harp, others a rose crowned; pretty and rare lot. 4 pieces
385 BRISTOL FARTHING, 1652; Thos. Butler, Merchant, Farthing; equally old and rare. 2 pieces
386 CHARLES II.; Irish half-pennies and "Carolus" farthings. 5 pieces
387 JAMES II.; Gun Money, crown of 1690, and varieties of the shilling and sixpence; very fine. 6 pieces
388 —— Similar, inferior to last. 4 pieces
389 —— Irish Revolutionary Coin; the "Floreat Rex" of the patriots, in circulation at the same time with the Gun Money; half-penny and farthings. 3 pieces

The following description of these curious pieces is copied from James Simon's Essay on Irish Coins, Dublin, 1749: "These half pennies have on one side the figure of a King crowned with a radiant crown, kneeling and playing on the harp, and over the harp the imperial crown of England, of a different metal, that is, brass upon copper, or copper upon brass, with this inscription, FLOREAT REX. Rev., the figure of St. Patrick mitred, and standing with a crosier in his right hand, and a leaf of trefoil in his left, which he holds out to the people about him; and on his left side, the arms of the city of Dublin, three castles. The farthings have on the reverse St. Patrick, mitred, holding in his left hand a double cross, a church behind him, and stretching out his right over a parcel of serpents as if driving them out of the church; inscription, ' Quiescat Plebs.' "

390 WILLIAM and William and Mary half-pennies and farthings; fair and good, rare.   4 pieces

391 ANNA; Farthing; very fine and rare, 1714.

392 GEORGE I.; Half-pennies and farthing, including Wood's issue.   4 pieces

393 GEORGE II.; Half-penny, 1749; bright and uncirculated.

394 —— Farthing, with the Isle of Man coins of his time.   5 pieces

395 VOCE POPULI Tokens, 1760.   4 pieces

396 GEORGE III.; Twopence, Penny, and Half-penny, with the raised rim and incused letters; fine, the penny nearly proof.   3 pieces

397 —— Penny, half-penny and farthing, 1806; a proof set, bright and uncirculated.   3 pieces

398 —— Farthing of same set, bright, and Irish farthing.   2 pieces

399 —— Bermudas Penny, 1793; fine proof, rare.

400 GEORGE IV.; Penny and half-penny and farthing; proof impressions, the penny turned on the edge by dropping; fine set.   3 pieces

401 WILLIAM IV.; fine uncirculated set, penny, half-penny, and farthing; bright.   3 pieces

402 —— Set, including half-farthing; very fine.   4 pieces

403 VICTORIA; Penny, half-penny, and farthing; bright and uncirculated.   3 pieces

404 —— Another set, equally fine.   3 pieces

405 —— Model Coins and Medalets of royal children; the coins running no lower than $\frac{1}{16}$ farthing, but the medalets down to a very small size.   8 pieces

Antique Coins. 27

406 VICTORIA and Jenny Lind medalets; reverses swan and Keep your temper; very fine. 3 pieces
407 COLONIAL Coins for the Canadas, Demarara, East India Co., Island of Jersey, Isle of Man, Ionian Islands, St. Helena, Barbadoes, etc., etc.; in the lot two electrotypes. 34 pieces
408 TRADESMEN'S Tokens; very fine, including Inverness half-penny proof, Druids, Coventry & Co. 10 pieces
409 —— Same; fine. 14 pieces
410 POLITICAL token of 1753; "The Speaker and Liberty;" obv. bust; rev. arms of Ireland, "The 124 Patriots, &c., Dec., 17, 1753;" very fine and rare.
411 KIRK'S Medalets and rare tokens. 5 pieces
412 MISCELLANEOUS English Coins. 65 pieces
413 CHOICE coins unclassified; one of Philip of Spain; one of a French Baron; Romulus and Remus Jeton; Henry V. Essay Coin, and one with a rooster, (Malacca). 5 pieces

AUTIQUE COINS.

Greek Silver.—Autonomous.

414 AEGNIA; Drachma (the oldest) Tortoise and incusum; a *good* example, rare.
415 ARGOS; forepart of a wolf; rev. in square incusum, A and crescent; drachm; very good.
416 ARCADIA; head; rev. AP I; below, Syrinx; fine and very rare type; Hemidrachm.
417 —— Head of Bacchus; rev. victory; fine drachm.
418 ATHENS; head of Minerva; rev. owl in a square incusum: to r. name of the city; to l. spray of olive; extremely fine tetradrachm in the thick form.
419 —— Tetradrachm, same type; very good.
420 AGRIGENTUM; vulture standing; above, name of the city; rev. in hollow, a crab; fine didrachm, and very rare.
421 —— Eagle flying with a hare in his talons; rev. Tripod and Ibis; A K R A in Greek letters; large didrachm; fine and rare.
422 —— Obolus; vulture and crab; fine and rare.

423 BŒOTIA; oval buckler; rev. in square incusum, vase (diota) and club; well preserved and rare drachm.
424 —— Drachm of the same type, but with the name of the City of Thebes, where it was coined; more rare than last and finer.
425 CHALCIS; female head; rev. eagle tearing a serpent; fine drachm.
426 CORINTH; head of Pallas; behind, olive branch; rev. Pegassus; very fine didrachm.
427 —— Duplicate, equally fine, but rusty.
428 HERACLIA; head of Pallas; rev. Hercules on his knees, struggling with a lion; hemidrachm; very good and rare type.
429 HISTIAE; head of a Bacchante crowned with ivy; rev. naked female sitting on the prow of a ship holding a sail; extra fine drachm.
430 —— Similar, equally fine.
431 —— Larissa, head of Apollo, full face; rev. a horse grazing; not absolutely perfect, but *fine*, and very rare didrachm.
432 MACEDONIA; first province under the Roman dominion; young female head to r., the hair flying; rev. within a laurel reath, club, table and altar: AESILLAS; beautiful tetradrachm; rare.
433 —— Female head, necklace and earrings; rev. prow of a ship; name, MAKE-NON; very fine and rare drachm.
434 NEAPOLIS; female head, N-E-P-O; rev. mask, with the tongue thrust out; fine and very rare drachm.
435 —— (In Campania modern Naples), head of the Syren, Parthenopeia, with necklace and earrings; rev. Victory crowning the Minotaur; in exergue, name of the city; a good didrachm of a rare type; rev. misstruck.
436 PHOCIS; bull's head, facing; rev. in square incusum, a boar's head; hemidrachm; rusty and imperfectly cleaned, but fine and rare.
437 SYRACUSE; head of Minerva, hair in net and fillet; around the head four dolphins; to r., name of the city; rev. Quadriga, the horses walking, Victory crowning them;

Antique Coins—Regal.

tetradrachm of a variety but rarely seen; full weight and fine.

438 SYRACUSE; Same in general, but with the legend *retrograde*, and on the reverse a *biga;* fine tetradrachm.

439 —— Tridrachm of the variety last described; very rare, but rubbed.

440 THURIUM; head of Pallas, with Syren on helmet; rev. a bull charging; in ex. fish, the name of the city above the bull; a fine and rare tetradrachm.

441 —— Head of Minerva, olive and helmet; rev. bull walking; in ex. fish, name of the city as before; well preserved didrachm; very rare.

442 THASUS; head of Bacchus crowned with ivy, hair long, no beard; rev. Hercules standing and inscription; broad and extremely fine tetradrachm.

443 TYRE; laureated head of Baal; rev. eagle and inscription; with the exception of a little rust, as it came from the die; rare tetradrachm.

444 VELIA; head of Pallas; rev. lion; didrachm.

445 HYLEA or ELEA; head of Pallas, with griffin and olive wreath on her casque; rev. lion springing on the back of a stag with long antlers; a beautiful didrachm, as it came from the die, and very rare.

446 INCERTA; head of Jupiter laureated; rev. within laurel wreath, cross and dolphin; very fine drachm.

447 UNCLASSIFIED drachms and hemidrachms, two of each. 4 pieces

448 DOUBTFUL tetradachm of base silver; obv. bust of Diana with bow and quiver; rev. eagle.

Regal.

449 ALEXANDER MAGNUS; head in lion's scalp; rev. Jupiter seated; very good example; tetradrachm.

450 —— Drachm, same type; *Extremely* fine.

451 —— Duplicate, fine.

452 ARIDÆUS (Philip), brother of Alexander; beautiful tetradrachm; hardly circulated; rare.

Antique Coins.

453 ANTIOCHUS III.; diademed head; rev. Apollo naked, holding an arrow and bow, seated on the cortina; his titles with monograms; nearly as it was coined; extra fine and rare tetradrachm.

454 —— VII. Evergetes; diademed head; rev. Minerva standing with Victory and lance; fine tetradrachm.

455 DEMETRIUS II. (Nicator), diademed head to r.; rev. eagle standing to l; palm club and various monograms; beautiful and rare tetradrachm.

456 LYSIMACHUS; diademed head, with horns of Jupiter Ammon; rev. Pallas seated; fine tetradrachm; very broad.

457 —— Same type. *Extra* fine tetradrachm.

458 PHILIP, father of Alexander the Great; bearded head of Jupiter, laureated; rev. young man with palm-branch, on a horse, the horse stepping to r.; extremely fine tetradrachm; rare.

459 —— Same; the horse stepping to left; splendid tetradrachm; very rare.

460 —— Drachma; beardless head; rev. same; fine.

461 PTOLEMY I. Soter; diademed head of Ptolemy to r., no beard; rev. eagle standing on a thunderbolt. Without marks of wear. Extremely fine tetradrachm, but struck a little to one side. Very rare.

462 —— Another fairly struck and very fine tetradrachm; same type.

Persian Coins.

463 ARTAXERXES ARDSHIR, A.D. 226, founder of the Sassanidan Dynasty; crowned or helmeted head, long braided hair and beard; rev. fire altar, inscription in characters, in appearance between the Samaritan and Greek Drachm; very fine and rare.

464 —— Or one of the same dynasty; rev. high altar attended by two priests. Size 16

Ancient Greek Copper.

465 EGYPTIAN KINGS and Roman Emperors; struck at Alexandria; curious and unusual reverses. 1st and 2d size; 12 pieces
466 CALES, Tauromenia, and Thurium; all well preserved and patinated. 3 pieces
467 RHODES, and divisions of the, as from cities of the Campania; fine lot. 4 pieces
468 MISCELLANEOUS. 8 pieces

Roman Consular Coins—Silver.

469 AEMILIA. Veiled head of Vesta—PAVLVS, &c.; rev. Lepidus and three prisoners beside trophy; in ex. PAVLLVS TER; very fine; rare.
470 ACILIA; laureated female head, SALVTIS; rev. Hygeia standing, AVILIVSV III IR; misstruck, but very fine.
471 CALPVRNIA; head of Apollo; rev. horseman riding at full speed, L. PISO, FRVGI; ex. fine.
472 CARISIA; head of Moneta; rev. implements for making coins—anvil, hammer, and pincers; misstruck, but little worn; very rare.
473 —— Head of Victory; rev. quadriga, T. CARISI; only fair.
474 CLAUDIA; head of Ceres, in field a lyre; rev. Diana holding two lighted torches; P. CLODIVS; good examples.
475 FLAMINIA; head of Rome; rev. L-FLAMIN-CILO; fine, rare.
476 FUFIA AND FURIA; two heads on each. 2 pieces
477 FURIA; Janus Bifrons; rev. Victory crowning a trophy; fine.
478 FONTEIA; Janus again; to r. star, to l. G; rev. a galley, C-FONT. ROMAS; large size, fair.
479 LUCRETIA; winged head; Victory to l.; rev. Dioscuri; very fine.
480 MARIA (?); head of Apollo; rev. two oxen in a plow; not worn; rare.

Antique Coins.

485 MANLIA; head of Rome; rev. Apollo (the sun) in his chariot—A. MANLI–Q. X; pierced; large size; rare.

486 MARCIA; head in a pileus (horned cap); rev. equestrian statue on an aqueduct, "Philippus;" notched with file, but fine and rare.

487 POMPEIA; head of Rome, behind Amphora; rev. fig-tree and black-birds, the shepherd Faustulus, with Romulus and Remus suckled by a she-wolf, SEX POM; fair, rare.

488 SERVILA; head of Rome to l., crown; rev. Castor and Pollux mounted, their horses starting in opposite directions—C-SERVILLI; good example; rare.

489 —— Another, the same; very fine, but the reverse misstruck.

490 SCRIBONIA; head of Fortune; rev. an altar, above, PVTEAL, below, SCRIBON; fine and scarce.

491 SULPICIA; veiled head (Vesta); rev. implements used in sacrifices, P. GALB–Æ–CV; fine.

492 —— Duplicate; fine.

493 THORIA; head of Juno, wearing a goat-skin head-dress, S. M–R; rev. Taurus Cornupetus, L. THORIVS–BALBVS; very fine.

494 TITIA; head of Bacchante; rev. Pegasus on a pedestal, Q. TITI; fine.

495 TITURIA; bearded head (Tatius); rev. rape of the Sabines; misstruck; fair.

496 VETURIA; head of Rome; rev. representation of the ceremony attending a treaty; called the "Alliance type;" very fair; rare.

497 VIBIA; head of Pan; rev. Jupiter seated, JOVIS. AXVR. C VIBIVS; fine.

498 UNCLASSIFIED; uncommonly good denarii.   5 pieces
499 —— Similar.   11 pieces
500 —— Quinarius; rare.

Antique Coins.

Roman Imperial Coins.

501 Caius Julius Cæsar, B. C. 47, denarius; elephant, CÆSAR; rev. five sacrificial implements; very fine.

502 —— Head of Venus; rev. Eunæas bearing Anchises and the Palladium, CÆSAR; a fine denarius, the obverse having been misstruck, so as to leave two distinct heads; rare.

503 —— Head of Julius; rev. winged Victory above the sacred chest, on each side a serpent erect—ASIA, RECEPTA; fine quinarius; rare.

504 —— Duplicate; fine.

505 Marc Antony, B. C. 47; bare head of Antony; rev. bare head of Octavius, CÆSAR IMP-PONT-III-VIR -R.P.C.; denarius in lead; fine and rare.

506 —— Galley; rev. standards; VII. legion.   2 pieces

507 Augustus, B. C. 31; denarius; rev. his grandsons, between them shields and religious implements; very fine.

508 —— Duplicate, very fine, but misstruck.

509 —— Another of this type, ordinary.

510 —— Bare head to left; rev. column supporting a radiated bust, IMP CAESAR below, thunderbolt; beautiful denarius, very rare.

511 —— First brass; rev. quadriga of Elephants; a fine example; rare.

512 —— Second size; bust; rev. AVGVSTVS; patinated, fine.

513 —— Same; head with spiked crown; rev. thunderbolt; very fine.

514 —— Same; rev. an altar, PROVIDENT; very fine.

515 —— Same; indifferent.   3 pieces

516 Tiberius, A.D. 14; denarius, head laureated; rev. female seated (Tribute penny); fine, scarce.

517 —— First brass; quadriga of Elephants; rev. S C and inscription; good example, very rare.

3

Antique Coins.

518 DRUSUS SENIOR, brother of Tiberius; bare head to l.; NERO CLAVDIVS DRVSVS GERMANICVS IMP; rev. Drusus seated on a pile of arms holding a sprig; fine, perfectly patinated, first brass; *very rare*, a valuable coin.

519 —— Duplicate; apparently finer, but tooled; very rare.

520 ANTONIA, wife of Drusus; bust; rev. figure standing, TI CLAVDIVS CAESAR AVG P M TR P IMP S C; perfectly patinated, and very fine and rare; second brass.

521 GERMANICUS, son of Drusus; head to l.; rev. S C; fully equal to last, same size; rare.

522 —— Obv. Germanicus in a quadriga; rev. SIGNIS RECEP DEVICT GERM S C; ordinary, but very rare; also second size.

523 CALIGULA, A.D. 37; head laureated, C CAESAR AVG GERMANICVS PON M TR; rev. three females standing, AGRIPPINA DRVSILLA JVLIA SC; an extremely rare first brass; an original coin, the obverse well tooled, the reverse untouched.

524 —— Second brass; rev. VESTA; extremely fine.

525 —— Same; poor.

526 AGRIPPINA, SENIOR, her head to r.; AGRIPPINA M F MAT C CAESARIS AVGVSTI; rev. a covered funeral chariot drawn by mules, MEMORIAE AGRIPPINAE; a fine large first brass; very rare and valuable.

527 CLAUDIUS, A.D. 41; head laureated to r.; TI CLAVDIVS CAESAR AVG PM TR P IMP; rev. a triumphal arch surmounted by an equestrian statue between two trophies; a rare first brass; the obverse *very* sharp and fine, the reverse weak; very desirable.

528 —— Obv. similar; rev. Hope standing; same size, fine.

529 —— Another of this type and size; perfectly patinated; fine and rare.

530 —— Second size; Ceres and warrior charging; both rare and in fair preservation.   2 pieces

Antique Coins. 35

531 NERO, A.D. 54; head laureated to r.; NERO CLAVD CAESAR AVG, etc.; rev. the Port of Ostia with vessels; above, a statue—below, a river god; fine first brass and very rare.
532 —— Obv. same; rev. Rome seated, S C; same size and equally well preserved.
533 —— Duplicate, except the head to l.
534 —— Varieties of second brass; no duplicates. 4 pieces
535 GALBA, A.D. 68; well patinated second brass; rev. Liberty; rare.
536 VITELLIUS, A.D. 69; head laureated to r.; rev. dolphin on a tripod, under the tripod a raven; denarius of the XV VIR (Quin-decemviri); very rare, but pierced.
537 VESPASIAN, A.D. 69; laureated head to r.; rev. female seated holding a sprig and caduceus, COS ITER, etc.; fine denarius.
538 —— Rev. TRI POT; seated figure; denarius.
539 —— Denarii of different reverses. 2 pieces
540 —— First brass of different types; very good. 2 pieces
541 —— Second brass; rev. the Genius sacrificing; patinated and fine.
542 —— Same size; rev. Judea Capta; fair, rare.
543 TITUS, A.D. 79; denarius; rev. Liberty; poor.
544 —— Laureated head to r.; IMP CAES VESP AVG PMT R PPP COS VIII; rev. three figures standing, PIETAS; fine and very rare first brass, tooled.
545 —— Laureated head to l.; rev. PAX; fine first brass.
546 —— Same; rev. S C figure standing; fine, same size.
547 —— Second size; varieties; fine lot. 3 pieces
548 —— First brass; Judea Capta; a good-looking coin, free from the ordinary marks of forgeries, but doubtful.
549 DOMITIAN, 81; denarius, laureated head; rev. IMP XIX COS XIIII Pallas armed passing to l.; beautiful; rare type.
550 —— Same; IMP XXI COS XVI; equally fine.
551 —— Same; Cos II; the Emperor on a horse; very rare.
552 —— Same; Minerva and owl on a prow; fine.

Antique Coins.

553 DOMITIAN; Same, Greek legend; rev. caduceus between two lyres, and others; fine lot. 9 pieces

554 —— First brass, Cos XI; rev. the Emperor in a military habit with a German shield, at his feet a woman kneeling, (probably signifying the submission of Germany); fine example, and very rare.

555 —— Second size, Cos XIIII; the Emperor sacrificing before a hexastyle temple, two musicians assisting; LVD SAEC FEC S C; good example, rare type.

556 —— Other second brass; fine. 2 pieces

557 —— First brass; rev. Mars and trophy; very good.

558 NERVA, A.D. 96; laureated head, IMP NERVA CAES AVG, etc.; rev. Modius with barley heads bending over the top, in the centre of the pot a poppy, PLEBEI VRBANAE FRVMENTO CONSTITVTIO S C. fine and extremely rare, first brass; struck to commemorate the celebration of the secular games.

559 —— Same; rev. two mules walking in opposite directions; VEHICVLATIONE ITALIAE REMISSA S C.; first brass, as fine and rare as the one last described.

560 —— Head with spiked crown; rev. two hands joined; very fine, second brass.

561 TRAJAN, A.D. 98, denarius, laureated head; rev. female standing with sprig and horn of plenty: Cos IV.; very fine.

562 —— Duplicate, equally fine.

563 —— Same; rev. Victory holding palm and crown; very fine.

564 —— Duplicate; fine.

565 —— Same; rev. Victory with trophy and crown passing to r.; fine.

566 —— Same; rev. Victory sacrificing; very fine.

567 —— Same; rev. Mars armed, holding a victory; very fine.

568 —— Same; rev. a column, on top statue, and others; good. 4 pieces

569 —— Same; rev. the Emperor seated, and same; rev. trophy and captive; fine. 2 pieces

Antique Coins. 37

62 570 TRAJAN; First brass; rev. Victory erecting a trophy of *H...*
           arms; fine, but not patinated; rare.
8 0 571 —— Same; rev. female with cornucopia and flower. *Horwit*
           fine.
10 572 —— Second size.   2 pieces *Ward*
. 2 573 HADRIAN, A.D. 117; denarius, laureated head; rev. a
           woman sitting on the ground holding a systrum, before *Fr. v*
           her an Ibis, AEGYPTOS; fine, and a rare and interest-
           ing type.
50 574 —— Same; rev. Victory with a trophy passing to r.; ex- *Barus.*
           tremely fine.
{ 575   —— Same; rev. Rome seated and female standing; fine.
                                                             2 pieces } *Ward*
{ 576   —— Duplicate of last lot.   2 pieces
   577   —— Denarii of Hadrian; good lot.   5 pieces
   578   —— First brass, laureated bearded head; rev. Hope *Authen*
           standing, SPES; patinated and very fine.
3 579   —— Same; bust with paludamentum and cuiras; rev. *Cook*
           warrior standing, VIRT AVC S. C.; patinated, fine
           and broad, very desirable.
15 580 —— Same; beardless head to left; rev. Justice seated; *cle*
           dark green patination, fine.
20 581 —— Same; laureated and bearded head to r; rev. the *Har*
           Emperor and attendants on an Estrade, a citizen re-
           ceiving gifts, LIBERALITAS AVG; a faint impression,
           perfectly preserved, patinated.
90 582 —— Same; rev. Pontifex Maximus; the Emperor seated *Balun*
           with hasta and Victory; perfectly patinated and pre-
           served.
10 583 —— Same; rev. female seated—"Indulgentia," etc.; *Cooke*
           extremely fine.
'0 584 —— Second size, head crowned; rev. Pegasus and others; *Quinn*
           some first size.   4 pieces
30 585 SABINA, wife of Hadrian; denarius; fair, scarce.
{ 586   —— First brass; head with high coif; poor.   } *Ward*
{ 587   —— Second size; perfectly patinated and fine, rare.
   588   AELIUS, son of Annius Verus and Rupilia Faustina; bare
0   head bearded; rev. figure passing to left; a good first *K*
           brass, not fine; rare.

Antique Coins.

589 Antoninus Pius, A.D. 138; denarius; laureated head rev. Modius with barley and poppy; fine; the planchet an irregular oval.

590 —— Same; rev. thunderbolt on a draped altar or table; fine.

591 —— Same; rev. a Priest sacrificing; extra fine.

592 —— Denarii; very good. 2 pieces

593 —— First brass, laureated and bearded head; rev. the Emperor in a gown (toga) sacrificing upon an altar, VOTA SVSCEPTA DECEN III. S. C.; in exergue Cos. IV.; light green patination, and *extremely* fine.

594 —— Same; rev. Apollo standing in the dress of a woman; in his right hand a patera, in his left a lyre, APOLIONI AVGVSTO; dark green patination, equally fine, and a very rare type.

595 —— Same; rev. the Emperor in a quadriga, COS IV.; very fine, rare type.

596 —— Duplicate of this rare coin; fine.

597 —— Same; rev. Fortune standing holding ears of barley and anchor, near her a Modius, ANNONA AVGG, S. C.; very dark patination; very sharp and fine.

598 —— Same; bare head of Antoninus; rev. a soldier carrying a man on his shoulder and leading another by the hand, the latter with a crooked staff, TRP COS III; extremely sharp and fine; *very rare*.

599 —— Same; rev. two figures seated within an octostyle temple with pointed gable, TEMPLVM DIV AVG REST COS IV.; not patinated, but nearly as it left the die; rare.

600 —— Same; rev. Romulus and Remus suckled by a she-wolf; very good, a little rubbed; rare.

601 —— Same; rev. on an Estrade, two Emperors seated on curule chairs, soldiers at each end; fair.

602 —— Same; rev. the Genius of the Roman Senate standing in a toga, GENIO SENATVS; fine.

603 —— Same; rev. Health standing feeding a serpent twined round an altar, SALVS; fine.

604 —— Same; rev. Fortune standing; fine.

ANTONINUS PIUS; First brass, with various reverses; all fine. 4 pieces
—— Same, bare head; rev. a four-story catafalque; patinated and well preserved.
—— Second size; two very beautifully patinated and fine. 4 pieces
FAUSTINA (the mother), wife of Ant. Pius; denarius, diademed head veiled, DIVA FAVSTINI; rev. Eternity personified; fine.
—— Same; rev. Priestess sacrificing; fine.
—— First brass; obv. bust of Faustina, DIVA, etc.; rev. Faustina holding a crown seated on the top of a car drawn by two lions, AETERNITAS S. C.; perfectly and beautifully patinated, light green, and almost as it left the die; very rare.
—— Same; rev. Faustina seated in a covered car drawn by elephants, same legend; a rare type, in fair preservation.
—— Second size; one very rare. 2 pieces
MARCUS AURELIUS, A.D. 161; denarius; head bare of young Aurelius Cæsar; rev. youth, JVVENTAS; very well preserved.
—— Same; head laureated of the Emperor; rev. the Emperor in the stola (sacred gown) sacrificing before a tripod altar, VOTA SOL DECENN COS III; very fine.
—— Same; rev. female seated holding balance and cornucopia; extra fine.
—— Same; rev. Mars with trophy; and another; fine. 2 pieces
—— First brass; head bare of Aurelius Cæsar; rev. Rome seated; patinated and fine.
—— Same; rev. Cæsar in a quadriga; same condition.
—— Same; laureated and bearded head of the Emperor Aurelius; rev. Victory erecting a shield or tablet, on which is inscribed, VIC. PAR; dark green polished patina, extremely fine on an irregular planchet.
—— Duplicate; very fine.

Antique Coins.

621 MARCUS AURELIUS; Same; rev. Rome seated on arms, holding a hasta; patinated and very fine.
622 —— Same; rev. female standing, with hasta and sprig; same condition.
623 —— Same; rev. a temple supported by four columns carved into terminal statues, the god within, the roof arched, the facade covered with bas-reliefs, FELIC AVC. Cos. III.; patination, a reddish brown; fine and extremely rare type.
624 —— Same; rev. two Emperors seated on an estrade and Liberality standing, a fourth figure mounting by a ladder, IMP. VIII., COS. IIII.; fine and extremely rare. (Havercamp, plate xix., RR.)
625 —— A variation of the same type, LIB AVGVSTOR T. R. P. XV., COS. III.; well preserved, rare.
626 —— Same; rev. eagle on a globe; patinated and fine.
627 —— Duplicate; nearly as fine.
628 —— Second size, head crowned; rev. VIC. PAR.; same as first size already described; rare and fine.
629 —— Same, head crowned; rev. thunderbolt; perfectly patinated and fine.
630 —— Same, laureated head; rev. female standing with a *tessare* and cornucopia; beautifully patinated and extremely fine.
631 —— First and second brass.   3 pieces
632 FAUSTINA, the daughter, wife of Aurelius; denarius; rev. female standing holding victory and a shield, AVGVSTI PII FIL.; very fine.
633 —— Duplicate and another, one pierced.   2 pieces
634 —— Same; rev. tomb, CONSECRATIO; good.
635 —— First brass, head of Faustina, hair in a knot low on the back of her head; rev. a mother, with two children in arms and two by her side, FECVND AVGVSTAE S. C.; dark green patination and very fine.
636 —— Same; diademed head, hair in braids and knot; rev. Happiness standing, LAETITIAE PVBLICAE; not patinated, but very fine.

Antique Coins. 41

637 FAUSTINA ; Same ; rev. Venus standing, VENVS ; same condition as last, rare.

638 —— Same ; rev. tomb, Cybele seated between two lions ; ordinary. 2 pieces

639 LUCIUS VERUS, associate of M. Aurelius ; laureated head bearded, IMP. CAES. L. AVREL. VERVS AVG. ; rev. young prince on horseback, with two attendants ; in ex., PROTECTION ; patinated and well preserved, a very desirable first brass, rare.

640 LUCILLA, wife of Verus ; denarius ; bust, hair waved and confined in a knot behind, LVCILLA AVGVSTA ; rev. Concord seated, CONCORDIA ; obv. fine.

641 —— Same ; rev. Venus standing ; very good.

642 —— First brass, draped bust ; rev. Venus standing ; beautifully patinated and extremely fine, also rare.

643 —— Second size, same ; rev. Juno standing, with hasta and patera, beside her a peacock ; beautifully patinated, fine and rare.

644 COMMODUS, A.D. 180 ; denarius ; laureated head ; rev. female standing holding a hasta and victory, NOBILIT AVG. PM. TR. PXI. IMP VIII., COS V. P.P. ; fine and *rare*.

645 —— Same ; rev. female standing holding sprig and cornucopia, TRP. VIIII., COS. IIII. ; fine, but dark.

646 —— First brass, laureated, bearded head ; rev. Cos XII., the Emperor in a toga, with patera and hasta ; perfectly patinated and fine, rare.

647 —— Same ; rev. Minerva charging ; equally fine.

648 —— Same ; rev. three females standing with balances and cornucopias (Moneta's) ; patinated and fine, also the type very uncommon.

649 —— Same ; rev. a heap of arms and armor, DE-GERMANIS ; a very fine and rare coin.

650 —— Another first brass of this rare type—not a duplicate ; equally fine and rare.

651 —— Same, bust in paludamentum and cuirass ; rev. tetrastyle temple, statue within, and one with light blue patination, good. 2 pieces

652 COMMODUS; Second size, crowned head; rev. trophy and two bound captives, DE-GERM; patinated, fine and rare.
653 —— Same; rev. Victory.
654 DIDIUS JULIANUS, IMPCAES. M DID SEPT SEVER JVLIANVS AUG.; rev. PM. TR. P. COS., Fortune standing holding a rudder and cornucopia; first brass, dark patination, and well preserved, very rare.
655 CLODIUS ALBINUS, second brass, laureated head; rev. COS. II., Æsculapius standing with his attributes; perfectly patinated and fine, very rare.
656 SEPTIMUS SEVERUS, A.D. 197; denarius; head laureated and bearded; rev. Victory standing writing on a shield resting on the trunk of a tree, PM. TR. P. XV. COS. III. P.P.; extremely fine, rare type.
657 —— Same; rev. the Emperor sacrificing, etc. 2 pieces
658 —— First brass, head laureated and bearded; rev. soldier holding hasta and victory; patinated and very fine, rare.
659 —— Second size, same type; equally fine.
660 —— First brass, two varieties; one having the edge upset before patination, forming a thick rim, "Consecratio" type; both fine. 2 pieces
661 JULIA DONNA, wife of Severus; draped bust, braided hair; rev. Venus standing half nude, leaning one arm on a short pillar, holding an apple and palm, VENERI VICTRIX S C; patinated and well preserved; first brass.
662 CARACALLA, A.D. 211; Denarius; head laureated and bearded; rev. Indulgence personified, seated on a high-backed chair; very fine.
662* —— Second brass; varieties. 2 pieces
663 GETA, brother of Caracalla; young head bare; rev. figure in a stola sacrificing; fine denarius.
664 —— Same; head laureated and bearded; rev. Fortune seated on the ground, one arm resting on a wheel, the other supporting a cornucopia, FORT RED TR, etc.; fine and rare type.

Antique Coins. 43

GETA; First brass; laureated and bearded head; rev. two Emperors (Geta and Caracalla) seated on curule chairs on an estrade, an attendant with cornucopia bestowing gifts, LIBERALITAS AVGG VI ET V; very fine and rare to excess.
—— Same; Victory seated; patinated.
MACRINUS, A.D. 217; first brass, in fair preservation; very rare.
ELEGABALUS, A.D. 218; denarius; rev. "liberality," "laetitia," "felicity," etc.; all fine.   4 pieces
—— Same; good reverse.   2 pieces
—— First brass; head laureated; rev. Peace with her attributes, PAX; patinated and fine. (Rare this size.)
JULIA MAESA, Elegabalus' Aunt; first brass, draped bust, braided hair; rev. Cybele seated between lions MATER; very good example; rare.
SEVERUS ALEXANDER, A.D. 222; first brass; laureated head; rev. Providence standing with her attributes; fine.
—— Duplicate of same; fine.
—— Same; rev. Rome seated; good.
—— Same; two varieties.   2 pieces
JULIA MAMAEA, mother of Severus; first brass; laureated head, hair in net; rev. Vesta holding a patera VESTA; perfectly patinated and fine.
MAXIMINUS, A.D. 235; denarius; laureated bearded head; rev. Peace standing holding hasta and flower; as it came from the die; rare.
—— First brass; same type; patinated and extremely fine; in this condition rare.
—— Same; rev. Victory; fine.
GORDIAN III., A.D. 238; first brass; laureated head, short hair; rev. female standing holding scales and cornucopia SECVRITAS AVC; patinated and fine.
—— Same; others of different reverse.   2 pieces
—— Denarius; rev. Victory; fine.
PHILIP SENIOR, called the Arabian, A.D. 244; laureated bearded head; rev. young prince on horseback; patinated and fine; first brass, rare.

Antique Coins.

684 TREBONIANUS GALLUS, A.D. 251; first brass; good, rare.
685 TRAJANUS DECIUS, A.D. 249; denarius; head in spiked crown; rev. Genius standing; fine.
686 VOLUSIANUS, A.D. 253; denarius; head in spiked crown; rev. Soldier standing VIRTVS AVG; extremely fine.
687 —— First brass; laureated head; rev. Concord standing; dark green patination, and extremely fine; rare.
688 VALERIAN, A.D. 253; first brass; laureated head without beard; rev. female standing with caduceus and cornucopia; patinated and very fine; rare.
689 —— Same; rev. Victory; equal to last; rare.
690 MARINIANA, wife of Valerian; veiled head; rev. peacock with tail spread; denarius; fine.
691 —— Second brass; same type; perfectly patinated and fine; rare.
692 POSTUMAS, Maximanus, Gordian III., and other billon; denarii. 10 pieces
693 GALLIENUS, Salonina, Julia Pia, Valerianus, and others; billon. 10 pieces
694 SIMILAR to last. 10 pieces
695 CLAUDIUS Gothicus, Tetricus, Mariniana, Gallienus, and others. 10 pieces
696 COPPER OF THEODOSIUS, Carausius (of Britain); Diocletian, Maxentius, Licinus, and others; fine and rare lot. 20 pieces
697 CONSTANTINE Family and others. 22 pieces
698 MISCELLANEOUS Ancient Copper Coins; some very rare ones in poor condition, as for example, one with the amphitheatre of Titus on the reverse. 50 pieces
699 MEDALLION of Marcus Aurelius, and first brass of Galba; rare types and finely executed modern counterfeits. 2 pieces
700 BRUNDUSIUM in Calabria; Greek copper coin of the second size; obv. laureated head of Neptune, behind trident; rev. Arion astride of a dolphin, lyre and victory in hand BRVN; in good preservation; very rare.
701 ANTIOCHUS VIII., Egypt; radiated head; rev. eagle thick copper; fine.

Copper Coins, Tokens, and Cards.

702 SIMON (JUDEA); grapevine; rev. pot of manna; fine example, sometimes called the "widow's mite;" an interesting and rare little copper coin.

703 JUDEA OF AUGUSTUS; obv. head; rev. hand grasping barley and poppies; fine little copper coin; rare.

704 TRIENS, third part of the As; obv. thunderbolt; rev. dolphin; thick copper, two inches broad, a piece broken off; very rare.

Addenda to Part I.

COPPER COINS, TOKENS, AND CARDS.

705 ITALY, 10, 5, 2, and 1 Centesimi, scarce as a set. 4 pieces
706 —— 5, 2, 1 and ½ Baiocchi, do. do. 4 do.
707 —— Soldi, 3 and 1 Centesimi, Napoleon. do.
708 SPAIN, different denominations of Isabella II., scarce. 3 pieces
709 FRANCE, Dix, Cinq, Deaux, and Un Centimi, Nap. III. 4 pieces
710 BELGIUM, 20, 10, and 5 Cents, Leopold, (nickel). 3 do.
711 —— 5, 2, and 1 Cents, Leopold, copper. 3 do.
712 FRENCH Republic, 1871, 10, and 5 Centimes. 2 do.
713 SIBERIA Cent, 1833 and 1847. 2 do.
714 CEYLON, 1802, (Elephant), scarce.
715 PERU Republic, 1864, 2 and 1 Centavo, Nickel 2 do.
716 LIMA Republic, 1855, Medio Centime.
717 VICTORIA Pennies, 1841 and 1874. 2 do.
718 —— Model Penny, and half Farthing. 2 do.
719 WOOD'S Half-pennies. 2 do.
720 JAPANESE Tempo.
721 VARIOUS copper coins; some rare. 15 do.
722 CANADA and others, two rare. 8 do.
723 CARDS, Apollo Gardens, Hess and Speidel. 2 do.
724 JENSON, Bell Founder, Chicago, scarce card.
725 BOLEN'S Card, (C. & W. M.) 2 do.
726 EVANS & WATSON.
727 R. LOVETT Jr's. Card, (Head of Penn.)
728 WORCESTER St. R.R., rubber.

46   *Copper Coins, Tokens, and Cards.*

729 CARDS, no duplicate; some scarce.   20 pieces
730 FRENCH Coins;   do.   8 do.
731 MISCELLANEOUS Coins.   25 do.
732 LINCOLN, 1860, W. M., scarce.
733 DOUGLASS & JOHNSON, Bell & Everett, and Breckenridge and Lane.   3 pieces
734 U. S. GRANT.
735 GRANT & COLFAX; rubber, scarce.
736 FRANKLIN Press Token, 1794, scarce.
737 MAP of France, 1794, scarce.
738 END of Pain, 1793, scarce.
739 —— Duplicate.
740 PIDCOCK's Token, scarce.
741 —— Duplicate.
742 SIX-AND-A-HALF Pounds of Bread for 1s., April, 1796; "God be Praised;" extremely rare token.
743 ODD FELLOW's Token, scarce.
744 LEED's Half-penny, proof, (1793), ex. fine, rare.
745 E. I. Co., do. do. do. 1791, scarce.
746 P. RATLEY, do. do. do. 1795, rare.
747 GRENDON, do. 1812, rare.
748 ROMULUS & REMUS, etc.   2 pieces
749 CENTS, 1794, 1796, 1798, 1802, 1803, 1816, 1817, 1818, 1819, 1820, 1825, 1826, 1827, 1829, 1830, 1831, 1833, 1837, 1838, 1840, 1842, 1853, 1854, and 1856. 25 pieces

Silver Coins.

750 HALF-DIME, 1795.
751 —— 1797.
752 DIME, 1846.
753 VICTOR EMANUEL; 50 and 20 Centesimi.   2 pieces
754 NAPOLEON; 10 Soldi, Italy, scarce.
755 PIUS IX.; 10 do.
756 SPAIN; two Reals, Isabella II.
757 TURKISH Coins, small.   3 do.
758 NAPOLEON II.; 50 Centimes.
759 DENMARK, William II., 25 and 10 Centimes.   2 do.
760 —— William III., 10 and 5 do.   2 do.

American Silver. 47

DEMARARA Half Guilder, George III.; scarce.
—— do., William IV.; do.
HONG KONG; 10 Cent Victoria.
VICTORIA, 1½ Penny; William III., 1½ penny. 2 pieces
WILLIAM I., Penny; broken.
HENRY III.; Penny.
SHILLING Token, 1812, Lancashire, etc.
SOUTH WALES, Bristol, etc., 12 pence, 1811.
CHARLES XI., Denmark, 2 marks, 1669; rare.
VARGAS Dollar. Mexico; rare.

AMERICAN SILVER.

Quarters.

1821 and 1825. 2 pieces
1860, Proof.
1860, Uncirculated.
1862, do
1862, Proof.
1863, do
1863, Uncirculated.
1864, Proof; scarce.
1865, Uncirculated; scarce.
1866, Proof; scarce.

Dimes.

1858, Proof; rare.
1859, do
1860, do
1862, do
1863, do
1864, do
1864, Uncirculated.
1865, Proof.
1866, Uncirculated.
1867, do
1869, do
1870, do

48   *American Coins.*

Half-Dimes.

793 1859, Proof.
794 1860, do
795 1862, do
796 1862, Uncirculated.
797 1864, do
798 1864, Proof
799 1866, Uncirculated; scarce.
800 1867, do do
801 1869, do
802 1870, do
803 1871, do

Three Cents.

804 1859, Uncirculated.
805 1860, do
806 1861, do
807 1861, Proof.
808 1862, Uncirculated.
809 1864, do
810 1864, Proof.
811 1865, do
812 1867, do
813 1870, do

Cents.

814 1860, 1862, 1864, 1865, 1866, all proof.

Two Cents.

815 1864, 1865, 1866, all proof.
816 1865, Three cents; proof.

Five Cents.

817 1866, 1866, 1866, all proof.

ANCIENT SILVER COINS.

818 ATHENS; thick tetradrachm, head of Minerva; rev. owl and spray of olive within a square incusum; fine.

819 TYRE; same; obv. head laureated (Baal?); rev. eagle, club, and palm-branch, Greek inscription; very fine and rare.

820 —— Duplicate; same in all respects.

821 THASUS; fine broad tetradrachm; obv. head of the Indian Bacchus; rev. Hercules standing, nude with the exception of the lion's skin hanging on his arm, his head laureated, the legend in Greek, "Hercules, Saviour of the Thasions; a beautiful example, in some respects the finest that I have seen.

822 CORINTH; Didrachm of the usual type—helmeted head and Pegasus; very good.

823 DIDRACHM; obv. helmet, TEM; rev. tripod and club; very fine and rare.

824 —— Head of Jupiter Dodonœus; rev. eagle on a thunderbolt, in Greek letters APEIROTAN, all inclosed in wreath of oak-leaves; fine and rare.

825 —— Persian of Artaxerxes; rev. fire altar; pierced.

826 ALEXANDER MAGNUS; Drachm of the usual type; good.

827 GREEK Imperial Tetradrachm of Heliogabalus, bust; rev. eagle holding a wreath; fine and rare.

828 MARCUS AGRIPPA, son-in-law of Augustus; silver coin of the usual type of his well-known copper; second size; obv. head; rev. Neptune standing; in excellent preservation and unknown rarity, his denarius being worth 200 francs; guaranteed original.

829 AUGUSTUS CÆSAR; Denarius, head laureated; rev. temple tetrastyle; fine and rare.

830 ANTONY; head of Cleopatra; rev. lion ANTON IMP; hemidrachm or quinarius; ordinary for condition, but very rare; and another. 2 pieces

831 CONSULAR Denarii; good. 6 pieces

832 IMPERIAL Denarii of Trajan, Antoninus Pius, and Septimus Severus. 3 pieces

50 *Modern Silver Coins.*

Ancient Copper Coins.

833 TRIENS; third of the as libralis; ● ● ● ◐ and thunderbolt; rev. ● ● ● ● and dolphin. Size 32
834 SEXTANS; half of last; ● ● and head of Mercury; rev. same and prow. Size 18
835 —— Same, with head of Mercury and two globules on both sides; same size.
836 UNCIA; the half of the sextans, or piece of one ounce; helmeted head and ●; rev. same and prow. Size 16
837 —— Same; a marked variety. Size 18

[These are divisions of a very early form of the AS, and are fine and valuable examples].

838 FIRST BRASS of Ant. Pius and Faustina the Elder. 2 pieces
839 —— Same of Marcus Aurelius and Faustina the daughter. 2 pieces
840 —— Same, of Hadrian, Commodus, and Gordian III. 3 pieces
841 SECOND SIZE of Nemauses, Augustus, and Agrippa; rev. crocodile chained to a palm tree, and others. 3 pieces
842 LARGE and small brass. 14 pieces
843 SMALL brass coins of the lower empire, from Constantine downward, with labels, fitted in a perforated card, good for a new collector. 40 pieces
844 PADUAN Copies or Forgeries of rare Medallions of Sept. Severus, Didius, Julianus, Helvetius Pertinax, and Plautilla; and one in the Contorniatus style of Domitian and Empress, which may be antique; making a fine lot of 5 pieces.

Modern Silver Coins.

845 CROWN of Frederick III., King of Denmark, Norway, and Sweden, 1660; crowned bust; rev. lion, DOMINVS PROVIDENT; very broad; a fine and scarce coin.
846 CROWN of the City of Mentz, 1639; rev. St. Stephen, PROTO MARTIR; broad, very fine and rare.
847 —— of the Republic of Venice, 1756; rev. "Franc, Lauredano Duce;" fine and rare.

Modern Copper Coins.

MEDAL of Aloysis Mocenigo Doge, 1766 ; rev. lion and tiger regarding each other, ARUM AFFRI in exergue; well preserved, very rare.   Size 20
CROWN of Louis XVI. France, 1783 ; mint mark, fox ; nearly uncirculated, scarce.
DOLLAR of Tunis ; very fine and rare.
HENRY II. of France, 1557 ; Testoon with his bust to the waist ; *extremely* fine, rare.
CHARLES, Duke of Nance ; Testoon, with bust ; same style and era ; very fine and rare.
LOUIS XIII., Quarter Crown, 1643 ; head laureated, bust draped in the Roman manner ; remarkably fine.
LOUIS XIV. ; without bust, 1645, arms crowned ; rev. cross ; equally fine, same size.
LOUIS XIV. and XV. ; Elizabeth of England and others ; small coins, $\frac{1}{16}$ crown average value ; a good lot.
    12 pieces
INDIFFERENT lot good silver and base coins.   12 pieces
REPUBLIC of Honduras ; nickel coins, $\frac{1}{2}$ and $\frac{1}{4}$ Reals, 1870 ; extra fine, rare.   2 pieces
MEDALET ; Napoleon, Eugenie, and the young Prince ; 3 busts, by Caque ; fine and uncirculated, rare. Size 10

Modern Copper Coins.

FRANCE ; a collection of value, comprising Old Baronial and Regal, Colonial and Revolutionary ; with Medalets of Napoleon I. and " Henri de France," Pretender, in unusually fine condition.   30 pieces
RUSSIA ; from 5 to 1 Copeck ; very fine.   7 "
TURKEY ; proof set ; beautiful, from size 12 to 24 ; desirable.   5 pieces
AUSTRIA ; Pieces of necessity of Francis I., 1807 ; 30, 15, and 16 krs. ; fine.   3 pieces
MISCELLANEOUS Medals and Coins, penny size ; a valuable lot.   12 pieces
—— Different sizes ; good lot.   12 "
ENGLISH half-penny tokens, many bright, with varieties of Lady Godiva, etc.   44 pieces

866 BAG of Old Coins, unclassified and generally poor, containing, however, some fine and uncommon pieces.
235 pieces

867 UNITED STATES Cent of 1793; rev. ONE CENT within an endless chain; rather poor; very rare.

868 —— of 1794; poor.

869 ROMAN, Emperors Gallienus and Tetricus; silver and copper. 3 pieces

870 —— Hadrian; rev. Galley, "Cos III.;" very fine medallion; copy of an antique; brass.

871 —— Vespasian; rev. "Judea Capta;" fine first brass; a little doubtful, but with the balance of probabilities on the side of its antiquity; if genuine, valuable.

872 BRONZE Medal of Frances Henry Egerton, Earl of Bridgewater. Size 28

873 —— Benj. Franklin; from the series Numismatica, by Durand. Size 28

874 —— Georgius Washington; same series.

875 —— General Lafayette; rev. "The Defender of American and French Liberty;" by *Caunos*. Size 32

876 PENNY of Victoria for New Brunswick, 1843.

PART II.

AMERICAN COINS.

Colonial.

877 ROSA Americana, 1723; Two penny (penny size), with the rose crowned; a beautiful and strictly uncirculated coin; rare.

878 —— Penny (half-penny size) of the same type and date; uncirculated; good companion to last; rare.

879 —— Same; with the rose without the crown, 1722; very good example.

880 —— Half-penny (farthing size), same date and type; copy; very fine.

American Coins. 53

881 WOOD Half-penny, 1723; beautiful, uncirculated example, with the harp *behind* the figure of Hibernia; rare.
882 —— Farthing, same date and type; uncirculated.
883 —— Duplicate, equally fine.
884 —— Half-penny; ordinary.
885 LOUISIANA Cent, 1721; letter L's back to back crossed under a crown; very fine, rare.
886 —— Cent of 1767; two sceptres crossed; rev. 3 lilies within a wreath, the two ends of the wreath touching a crown; a beautiful uncirculated example, nearly proof; very rare.
887 —— The same, with RF stamped over the lilies by a punch; extremely fine.
888 RHODE Island Medal, 1773, map; rev. Adm'l Howe's flagship; brass; extremely fine.
889 CONTINENTAL Currency, 1776; fine original in tin; scarce, spelled currency; extremely fine, rare.
890 GEORGIUS Triumpho, 1735; good example.
891 LOUISIANA, Franklin, Mott, and Talbot, Allum and Lee Cents. 5 pieces
892 TALBOT, ALLUM & LEE Cent, of 1794; NEW YORK above the ship; uncirculated; rare.
893 —— The same, muled with the BIRMINGHAM HALF-PENNY; a brilliant proof impression; very rare.
894 —— Same of 1795; NEW YORK in the legend, around the ship; uncirculated and bright; rare.
895 FRANCO-AMERICANA (Castorland) Token; fine proof copper.
896 IMMUNIS COLUMBIA, 1787; a fine uncirculated impression; *very rare.*
897 NOVA CONSTELLATIO, 1783, with small letters and large script; two examples, almost uncirculated; very desirable. 2 pieces
898 —— Repetition of last; very good pair. 2 pieces
899 MASSACHUSETTS Cent, 1787; good impression, but little worn, but dark.
900 —— Half Cent, same date; strictly uncirculated piece; rare.
901 —— 1787 and 1788; a pair, rather poor. 2 pieces

54 American Coins.

902 ENGLISH HALF-PENNY, with a Massachusetts Indian with tomahawk and bow. "If rents I once consent," etc. uncirculated; rare.
903 NEW JERSEY Cents, 1787; varieties in the horses heads and shape of ploughs; very nearly uncirculated. 3 pcs
904 —— Another selection; fine. 3 pieces
905 —— Similar. 3 pieces
906 —— With broad planchets, above the plough, a trefoil; extra fine; rare.
907 —— Same, with two small do. 4 pieces
908 —— With horse head to left; a rare type, and although dark, and not a strong impression, but little worn and desirable.
909 CONNECTICUT Cents; laureated head to left; uncirculated impression, 1788; rare.
910 —— Same, very fine; varieties. 3 pieces
911 —— With head to right; nearly uncirculated; rare.
912 —— Heads to right and left; some fine. 5 pieces
913 —— And New Jersey. 8 do.
914 VERMONT Cents; good. 2 do.
915 COLONIALS, unclassified. do.

Cents.

916 WASHINGTON Cent, 1791, large eagle; bright and uncirculated; nearly proof, and in reality more rare than the *small* eagle variety.
917 1793, Wreath; small date, good color; fair Cent.
918 1793, Same, small planchet; poor.
919 1794, Large planchet; broad milling; fine.
920 1794, Small do., broken die, dark, but very good.
921 1795, Plain edge, dark; very good Cent.
922 1794, '95, '97, '98, and 1800; from poor to fair. 5 pieces
923 1798, 1800, and 1802; dark, but very fair. 3 do.
924 1803, Good color and sharp; not uncirculated.
925 1804, Dark and rubbed, but not very poor; rare.
926 1805, A good Cent for date.
927 1806, Also good for date; not fine.
928 1806 and 1809, poor; scarce. 2 pieces
929 1810, Two varieties, and 1811, fair. 3 do.

American Coins. 55

930 1812, Better, very good Cent.
931 1814, Extremely fine, stars sharp; fine color.
932 1814 and 1815, but with some doubts as to whether the last date is correct; it looks like a typographical error. 2 pieces
933 1816, Broken die; uncirculated and bright.
934 1817, Uncirculated; much fine red color remaining.
935 1817, Uncirculated; not bright.
936 1818, Good color, and nearly uncirculated.
937 1819, Uncirculated; bright red.
938 1820, Same.
939 1820, 1821, and 1823, all poor. 4 pieces
940 1823, Poor, but scarce.
941 1824, Fine.
942 1830, Only fair, the reverse fine.
943 1831 and 1833, fine Cents. 2 pieces
944 1834, Uncirculated; fine color, hardly tarnished; very desirable.
945 1838, Uncirculated; red.
946 1838, Same; fine olive brown.
947 1840 and 1841, very good. 2 pieces
948 1843 and 1846, do. 2 do.
949 1846, Uncirculated.
950 1847 and 1848, good Cents. 4 pieces
951 1848 and 1849, uncirculated. 2 do.
952 1849 and 1859, fine. 2 do.
953 1850, '51, '52, '53, and '54, uncirculated and bright. 5 pcs
954 1855, Upright and oblique date, do. do. 2 do.
955 1857, Large and small date; fine. 2 do.
956 1856 and other 50's, generally bright. 8 do.

Half Cents.

957 1803, '4, '6, '7, and '9, all but first two very fine. 5 pieces
958 1828, '29, and '32, good 3 do.
959 1833, '34, and '35, uncirculated. 3 do.
960 1851, '53, and '56, very fine. 3 do.
961 VARIOUS dates. 11 do.
962 NICKEL from 1857 to '64 inclusive; uncirculated. 8 do.

56　　　　　　　　*American Coins.*

963 COPPER, nickel size, from 1864 to 1873 inclusive. 10 pcs
964 ——— Two Cents, from 1864 to 1870 inclusive. 8 pieces

Proof Sets.

The following will be found in the same condition as when delivered at the mint, and in the same wrappers; they are small sets, 5 and 3 cent pure nickel, and 2 and 1 do. copper.

965 1867, Four pieces.
966 1868, Same.
967 1869, do.
968 1870, do.
969 1871, do.
970 1872, do.
971 1873, do. very rare.

The remaining proof sets contain, besides the "small set," the dollar, half and quarter dollar, dime and half dime, making 10 pieces.

972 1866, Ten pieces.
973 1869, do.
974 1870, do.
975 1872, do.
976 1874, Nine pieces.

Pattern Pieces.

977 DOLLAR of 1836; artist's name on base of the figure of Liberty; tarnished proof; rare.
978 FIRST steam coinage, 1836, (March 23); bronze proof, scarce.
979 CENT of 1854; head of Liberty without legend, and same date, with flying eagle within circle of stars; proof. 2 pieces
980 ——— of 1855, flying eagle (like last); trial of copper and nickel. 2 pieces
981 ——— Set of the patterns offered in 1858 for nickel Cents, viz.: four with Indian head; rev. oak wreath and shield, oak wreath without shield, laurel wreath and old wreath; four with *small* eagle, and the same reverses, and four with *large* eagle and same; making a proof set of twelve pieces.

American Coins.

982 HALF DOLLAR of 1869, STANDARD SILVER; head diademed; brilliant proof.
983 —— Head with star, brilliant.
984 —— Same in phrygian cap; brilliant.
985 QUARTER DOLLAR, same date, diademed head; proof.
986 —— Head with star; proof.
987 —— Same in phrygian cap, proof.
988 DIME; same date; head with star; brilliant; proof.
989 —— Same in phrygian cap,   do.

Gold.

990 EAGLE of 1795; nearly uncirculated, but pierced; scarce.
991 HALF-EAGLE, small date; on rev. small eagle; extremely fine; in this condition, rare.
992 EAGLE, 1799; ordinary (good) condition.
993 EAGLE, 1801; remarkably fine; scarce.

Silver Dollars.

994 1794, Very good, the minting not sufficiently forcible to overcome the drift marks on the planchet, but every part of the dies fairly impressed; the head considerably worn, but on the whole a desirable dollar; very rare.
995 1795, Same type (head with flowing hair); very fine; rare.
996 1795, Fillet head; fine, very scarce.
997 1799, Uncirculated, with slight marks of friction against other coins in same bag.
998 1800, Very fine.
999 1801, Fine.
1000 1802, Equal to 1799, and with the same qualification, uncirculated; scarce.
1001 1803, Fine.
1002 1850, New Orleans mint, fine.
1003 1866, Brilliant proof.
1004 1870, Same.
1005 1871, Very fine.
1006 1872, Uncirculated.

1007 1873, Very fine.
1008 1873, "Trade dollar;" brilliant.
1009 1873, Duplicate.

Half-Dollars.

1010 1794, Considerably circulated, but not scratched; scarce.
1011 1795, *Uncommonly fine;* very rare.
1012 1801, Seldom found better, or even as good; but much circulated; scarce.
1013 1802, Same condition, and subject to same remarks; scarce.
1014 1803, Much finer; even *fine,* for date.
1015 1805, About like last, or very fair.
1016 1812, Nearly uncirculated; scarce.
1017 1823, Very fine.
1018 1830, Entirely uncirculated.
1019 1832, Very fine.
1020 1836, Uncirculated and brilliant; scarce.
1021 1838, Extremely fine.

Dimes.

1022 1796, Extremely fine; rare.
1023 1829, Uncirculated.
1024 1833, Extremely fine.
1025 1859, Brilliant proof.
1026 1860, Fine proof.
1027 1862, Same.
1028 1863, do.
1029 1866, do.
1030 1867, do.
1031 1868, do.
1032 1869, do.
1033 1870, do.
1034 1871, do.
1035 1872, do.

Half-Dimes.

1036 1794, Very fair; scarce.
1037 1829, Uncirculated.

American Coins. 59

1038 1836, Uncirculated.
1039 1832, Very fine.
1040 1847, Uncirculated.
1041 1850, Very fine.
1042 1851, Same.
1043 1852, do.
1044 1853, do.
1045 1855, do.
1046 1856, do.
1047 1857, do.
1048 1858, Fine proof.
1049 1859, Same.
1050 1860, Very fine.
1051 1861, Fine proof.
1052 1862, Scratched proof.

Personal and Political Medalets.—Silver.

1053 WASHINGTON, Siege of Boston, 1775 ; Washington on horseback; fine proof; Lovett's series.
1054 ——— North Point and Fort McHenry; bust; rev. monument in Baltimore ; fine proof.
1055 FREE TRADE and Sailors' Rights ; Lovett's series ; fine proof.
1056 FIREMAN'S Medal, 1860 ; fine proof.
1057 THE Loyal National League ; War of 1861; fine proof. Size 24
1058 SOCIETY Medal, engraved arms of New Jersey ; rev. member's name, loops; origin unknown. Size 20

In Copper, Brass, and Tin.

1059 WASHINGTON Cents of 1783, Unity States, and double head. 2 pieces
1060 ——— Washington and Independence, same date. 2 pcs
1061 ——— Liberty and Security ; large die ; uncirculated, rare.
1062 ——— Grate cent, 1795 ; uncirculated, scarce.
1063 ——— Wyon medal, 1796; history in three circles circumscribing cannon and Fasces, Caduceus and scroll ; very good, slight scratches ; scarce.

American Coins.

1064 WASHINGTON; Success to the United States; brass token, poor.

1065 —— C. Wolfe, Clark and Spies' card; with heads of Washington and Jackson, in oval rings; brass, much rubbed, but a rare piece.

1066 —— Bust; rev. born and died, etc., by Lovett; tin. Size 22

1067 —— Bust; below, SECURITY; rev. ship; after the Sommer Island piece; fine proof; copper, scarce. Size 22

1068 —— Similar; rev. (engraved) W. H. SMITH, Co. G. 11th Reg. N. Y. Volunteers, July 24; brass. Size 22

1069 —— Bust, full face; rev. "He is a Freeman whom the Truth makes free;" copper. Size 22

1070 —— Bust; rev. Brimlow's card; 2 (cents); copper and brass varieties; ex. fine. 5 pieces

1071 —— Patriæ Pater; VIRTUE, etc.; copper. Size 18

1072 —— Same; rev. born and died, head on both sides; fine proof, on ex. thick copper, planchet. Size 14

1073 SAGES' Historical Tokens; fine proof impressions in copper; Nos. 1, 2, 6, 10, 12, and 13. 6 pieces

1074 —— "Odds and Ends;" Nos. 1, 2, and 3; same style. 3 pieces

1075 —— "Numismatic Gallery;" "odds and ends," etc.; same style and condition. 4 pieces

1076 DAVID HOSACK; bust; rev. Arts and Science; fine proof, copper, by *Furst*. Size 22

1077 INDEPENDENCE HALL, 1776; rev. the Liberty Bell; splendid proof, copper. Size 24

1078 —— Same, in brass.

1079 CONTINENTAL Currency Seal, 1778; fine proof, copper, dollar size.

1080 STEPHEN GERARD, the benefactor of Philadelphia; fine proof, copper. Size 22

1081 FREE TRADE and Sailor's Rights, by *Childs*, Chicago; tin. Size 24

1082 SABBATH-School Jubilee, July 4, 1842, and Odd Fellows Hall; corner-stone laid, etc.; copper and tin, fine proofs; size 22 and 24. 2 pieces

American Coins.

1083 NASSAU Water-Works, and Temperance Medal ; fine tin proof pieces ; size 22 and 24. 2 pieces
1084 JOHN BULL to Brother Jonathan, and World's Peace Jubilee (Boston) ; cross ; copper and tin. 2 pieces
1085 GEN. GEO. B. MCCLELLAN ; Army Medal, by *Merriam ;* fine proof, copper. Size 22
1086 —— Bust, ¾ face ; rev. One flag, and one Union ; tin. Size 22
1087 —— Bust, to left ; rev. the People's Choice, 1864 ; copper and tin ; size 22. 2 pieces
1088 —— Same ; rev. The Constitution as it Is ; (McClellan and Pendleton) ; tin. Size 22
1089 —— Same ; rev. Washington's bust, surrounded by arms ; tin. Size 20
1090 —— Same ; rev. Eagle standing on a drum ; rubbed brass ; rare. Size 20
1091 —— Same ; rev. Monitor, 1862 ; fine proof, on thick planchet ; copper. Size 20
1092 ABRAHAM LINCOLN, bust ; rev. rail fence, " the great rail splitter," 1860 ; copper proof. Size 22
1093 —— " Honest Old Abe ; " rev. " Union Candidate," etc. ; tin. Size 20
1094 STEPHEN A. DOUGLASS, bust ; rev. eagle ; by *True ;* proof ; tin. Size 22
1095 GENL. U. S. GRANT, 1868 ; bust, three-quarter face ; rev. " I propose," etc. ; fine proof brass. Size 18
1096 —— 1872, " Presidential Candidate," etc. ; fine proof in tin by *Key.* Size 16
1097 ANDREW JOHNSON, " President 17th " ; tin medalet. Size 12
1098 MAJ.-GEN. ANTHONY WAYNE, (Robinson's Series) ; tin, silver-plated proof. Size 22
1099 BOMBARDMENT of Fort Sumter, April 12 and 13, 1861 ; thick planchet, copper proof. Size 22
1100 DICKESON'S Card ; rev. " Sommer Island XII ; " Hog standing ; nickel. Size 20
1101 HAVANA Express Card, and " I am ready," 1861. 2 pieces

1102 ANDREW JACKSON, Gen. Harrison, Henry Clay, Winfield Scott, Martin Van Buren, and Genl. Taylor; brass medalets. 6 pieces

1103 HARRISON Medal in white metal; rev. log cabin with tree and cider bbl. to left, flag flying across the house; poor. Size 22

1104 POLITICAL Cards, melanotypes, etc. 15 pieces

1105 COPPERHEADS; S. H. Zahm's card, (dealer in coins, Lancaster, Pa.), and others selected for rarity. 20 pieces

1106 —— Box containing a collection of 400 pieces.

1107 SHIN-PLASTERS, 1837–41; no duplicates; fine. 10 pieces.

1108 —— and Cards. 13 pieces

1109 —— Benton mint drop; uncirculated.

1110 —— Jackson, I take the responsibility, brass; rare.

1111 —— Same in copper; bright and uncirculated, with others in same condition; rare lot. 6 pieces

1112 METROPOLITAN Insurance Co.'s Card, etc. 5 pieces

American Medals.

1113 GEORGE WASHINGTON, Medal inscribed to his memory, by D. Eccleston Lancaster; bust; rev. Indian standing, circumscribed by legend in three circles; hacked and abused, although but little worn; copper. Size 48

1114 —— Medal by Westwood, bust to r.; rev. inscription in curving lines within a laurel wreath, the ends touching a bundle of arrows tied in the middle; much handled, and consequently tarnished, although not rubbed, copper. Size 28

1115 LAFAYETTE medal, by *Caunois*, 1825; "The defender of American and French Liberty;" splendid proof, copper. Size 32

1116 JOHN ADAMS, March 4, 1825, bust; rev. "Science gives Peace, and America Plenty;" illustrated by emblematical figures; soft metal, bronzed; original and very rare. Size 32

Coins of Mexico.   63

1117 DANIEL WEBSTER, bust; rev. monument, on its top a globe, on its base, "I still live," in case; fine proof copper; by *C. C. Wright*. 4.75 Hall

1118 —— Tin medal, bust; rev. Defender of the Constitution; rare. Size 24 75 Holland

1119 ANDREW JACKSON, for gallantry at New Orleans, Jan. 8, 1815; National, by *Furst*; fine proof; copper. Size 40 1.00 HnC

1120 ISAAC SHELBY, for services at the battle of the Thames, Oct. 5, 1813; National, *Furst;* fine proof. Size 40 1.37 do

1121 GEN. WINFIELD SCOTT, for gallant and successful service in the Mexican War; fine proof, bronze; *C. C. Wright*. Size 56 5.00 d.

1122 —— Presented by the Commonwealth of Virginia to her distinguished son, etc., for same campaign; by same. Size 56

1123 ERIE Canal Medal, "Union with the Atlantic," etc., 1826; tin, uncirculated. Size 30 50

1124 NEW YORK Crystal Palace, 1853; First Pillar erected Oct. 30, 1852; tin proof. *Dowler*. Size 32 75

1125 DR. ELISHA KENT KANE, Masonic medal, by G. H. Lovett; bronze proof. Size 32 60

1126 ABRAHAM LINCOLN, by *W. H. Key*; rev. broken column and flags, assasinated 14th April, 1865; thick planchet, splendid bronze proof. Size 34 1.00

1127 —— Same in tin. 20

1128 U. S. GRANT, *Bovy* (Geneva), obv. bust; rev. Patient of Toil etc.; splendid bronze proof, thick planchet. Size 38 1.00

1129 —— Bust; in ex., "The Oceans united by Railway, May 10, 1869," by *Barber;* splendid bronze proof. Size 30 65

1130 STONEWALL JACKSON, by *Caque;* tin. Size 32 35

1131 CONNECTICUT State Agricultural Society; rev. awarded to; bronze proof. Size 32

COINS OF MEXICO.

1132 COB Dollar, 1733; 8 Reals, very good. 1.75

1133 —— Same (1)758; clump form, pierced. 1.00

Coins of Mexico.

1134 Cob (or cut) half dollar, 1739.
1135 —— Fractions 1 and 2 Reals. 5 pieces
1136 —— of Caracas, 2 Rs.; very fine. 2 "
1137 Dollar of the Republic, coined at *Durango*, 1824; crooked necked eagle on a cactus, in his claws a serpent; good and rare.
1138 —— Duplicate, same mint, rubbed, but good; very rare.
1139 —— Same type, from the mint at Guanaxuato, a variety of the "Crook Neck" type; rubbed, but as good as usually found; very rare.
1140 —— Crook Neck dollar of 1825, from the same mint, larger planchet and finer, only the eagle and cap of Liberty (on the two sides), rubbed; very rare.

> The appearance here of *four* coins described as rare, requires the explanation, that *because* they are rare, this Collector has secured every dollar of this type that has come to his knowledge during all the years in which his cabinet has been forming.

1141 —— With eagle on a cactus, standing upright; from the Mint of *Durango*, 1834; has the appearance of having been cast; rare.
1142 Half Dollar of 1864, from the mint of *Zacatecas*; eagle upright, nearly proof, scarce.
1143 Maximilian Dollar, 1866; fine.
1144 —— Half do " "
1145 —— 10 cents, "
1146 —— 5 do "
1147 —— Copper Cent, 1864, "1 Centavo," not a good impression, but nearly uncirculated, and extremely rare.
1148 1872, Dollar of the Republic; "un Peso," from the mint of Zacatecas; brilliant.
1149 1870, Quarter Dollar (25 centavos), mint of Guanaxuato; very fine.
1150 Reals of the old and new Republics; very fine.
2 pieces

Bolivia. 65

SPANISH MEXICAN COINS.

1151 1745, Globe dollar of Philip V.; crowned shield and titles; rev. two hemispheres under a single crown, between the pillars of Hercules; nearly uncirculated, scarce.

1152 1746. Dollar of the same type, pierced; equally fine.

1153 1761. Quarter of the same type, Charles III.; very fine.

1154 PISTAREENS, various types and dates. 3 pieces

1155 1808, Pillar dollar of Charles IIII.; extremely fine— coined at *Tlalpan;* very rare.

1156 1819, Same of Ferdinand VII., coined at the *City of Mexico*, equally fine.

1157 —— Duplicate; very fine.

1158 BASE dollar of same, intrinsic value doubtful, rudely executed die, and much more rare than the good coins; has been much circulated.

1159· HAMMERED quarter-dollar from the Zacatecas mint, provisional money of 1811; crowned shield between pillars of Hercules; rev. cross on a mountain-top, the rest obliterated; very rare.

1160 PROCLAMATION half-dollar, 1843; "Jura de la Constitucion Mexicana;" rev. "Libertad," with loop; ex. fine and rare.

CENTRAL AMERICA.

1161 DOLLAR of 1824, chain of mountains, sun rising in splendor; rev. a tree; very fine.

1162 HONDURAS provisional money, 1851; copper, with coating of tin; varieties; very rare. 3 pieces

1163 —— Copper; 4 Ps. and 2 do, 1862; very fine. 2 pieces

BOLIVIA.

1164 DOLLAR of 1827, laureated bust of Simon Bolivar; rev. two llamas lying down under a tree; very fine and rare.

La Plata—Peru—Brazil.

1165 HALF-DOLLAR, same type; equally fine and rare.
1166 DOLLAR of 1865, bust of General Melgarejo; rev. inscription; ex. fine and rare.

LA PLATA.

1167 DOLLAR of 1815, coined at Potosi; sun; rev. "En Union y Libertad;" good, scarce.
1168 COPPER, "Cuatro Centavos; ex. fine, scarce. Size 24

PERU.

1169 DOLLAR of Cuzco, South Peru, 1838; sun and five stars; rev. castle and volcano; extremely fine, scarce.

BRAZIL.

1170 PETRUS II., 1695; two Patacs, 640 reis, arms of Portugal; rev. a belted globe on a cross; good, scarce.
1171 JOANNES, 1813; three Patacs, 960 Reis (crown), same type; very fine, scarce.
1172 —— 1820; different types of the same value; instead of the arms of Portugal, the denomination (960) and date within a wreath and crown; very fine, rare.
1173 PETRUS II., 1865; set of half-dollar, quarter-dollar, and dime (1,000, 500, and 200 Reis); uncirculated. 3 pcs
1174 —— Nickel coins, 200 and 100 Reis; very fine. 2 pieces
1175 JOSEPH I., John V., Peter I., John VI., Michael I., and Maria II., coppers of Brazil and Portugal, 80, 40, 20, and 10 Reis, all fine and without counter-stamps; a valuable series, from size 16 to 28. 10 pieces
1176 —— Similar, but inferior. 10 "
1177 —— Another lot; poor. 10 "
1178 CHILI, Brazil, Buenos Ayres, and Venezuela copper coins. 8 pieces

WEST INDIA ISLANDS, AFRICA, &C.

CURACAO 1821; beautiful little coins of this Island, 1 REAL; uncirculated. 2 pieces

CARACAS and Guiana; a collection of uncirculated coppers, rarely seen. 20 pieces

DOMINICAN Republics, 1848; brass "$\frac{1}{4}$," rare; another brass token MITAD, etc.; rare lot. 4 pieces

PARAGUAY $1\frac{1}{2}$, 1845, lion guarding a liberty pole; extra fine, copper. Size 15

ANTIGUA farthing, palm tree; fine, rare.

BERMUDA penny, George III., 1793; fine, rare.

BAHAMA penny (half-penny size), 1806, Gibraltar "2 Quartos," and Centavo of Peru. 3 pieces

ST. HELENA and East India Co. half-pennies. 2 "

BARBADOES, the two varieties, pennies, fair; 2 pieces; with President Geffrard Haite, 3 pieces.

LIBERIA half-penny, and Macuta of Africa, under Joseph I. of Portugal, 1763; the latter very rare, fine.
3 pieces

MOHAMMEDAN coins and lead tokens of the class said by Payne Knight to have been found in the River Seine; very interesting and rare. 6 pieces

EAST INDIA Co. and South American copper coins.
50 pieces

COINS OF ENGLAND.

Silver.

HENRY II. penny, head, full face; rev. double cross, little crosses in the angles; very good. 2 pieces

EDWARD I., Irish penny, head in a triangle; rev. long cross, with pellets in the angles; fair, rare.

CHARLES I. Shilling (Plate XIX. No. 12, Ruding); stained, but very perfect; rare type.

JAMES II., crown 1688; a little stained and slightly rubbed, yet desirable; rare.

English Coins—Copper.

1195 ANNA; "Vigo" crown, 1703; very fine; nearly uncirculated.

1196 GEORGE I.; very fine crown of 1715; obv. laureated bust, with titles; rev. motto and arms of England, with the horse of Hanover on one quarter of the shield, BRVNS, ET LVNE DVX, etc.; rare.

1197 GEORGE III; St. Andrew crown for Br. and Lun, 1769; very good, rare.

1198 —— Another; different types; obv. bust in the Roman manner; rev. same as on the Brunswick crown of George I., just described; very fine, rare.

1199 —— "Two-third" thaler; same, 1814; extra fine.

1200 VICTORIA florin, 1849; "Dei Gra" omitted; very fine and rare.

1201 —— Same of 1851; very fine.

1202 —— Dollar for Hong Kong; fine.

1203 —— Half-dollar   do   equally fine.

1204 PETERBOROUGH Bank Token, 1811; rev. Cathedral; fine proof shilling token, with the Dundee shilling token; not fine, but very rare.   2 pieces

Maundy Money.

1205 WILLIAM and Mary; full set; 4d, 3d, 2d, and penny; nearly all very fine; rare.

1206 ANNE; beautiful; uncirculated set; rare.

1207 GEORGE III; young head; same; rare.

1208 GEORGE IV.; proof set; rare.

1209 WILLIAM IV.; proof set; rare.

1210 VICTORIA; same, 1853.

1211 —— 4d, 3d; uncirculated.   4 pieces

Copper.

1212 CHARLES II.; Irish half-penny, 1681; fine.

1213 JAMES II.; gun money; crown, shilling, and sixpence, 1690; and "Voce Populi" half-penny, 1700; very rare.   4 pieces

Coins of France—Silver.

1214 KILDARE Token or Medal, penny size; obv. Kildare guarding treasure, TOUCH NOT SAYS KILDARE, 1755; rev. harp crowned, PROSPERITY TO OLD IRELAND, 1754; brass, in very good condition; very rare.

1215 TAUNTON Farthing, 1667; "By the Constable;" rev. a ton across the letter T; brass, in fair preservation, and extremely rare.

1216 FARTHINGS of William I., William and Mary, George I., II., III., and IV., William IV., and Victoria, with model coins, Jetons, etc.; a mixed lot; some very fine, some poor. pieces

1217 GEORGE III. two-pence; poor; "Hide and De Carle," Melbourne; token in commemoration of the coronation of George IV., and half-penny tokens.
10 pieces

1218 VICTORIA Penny, half-penny, and farthing; the two styles; sets of each; uncirculated. 6 pieces

1219 TRADESMEN'S Tokens; half-penny, and farthing size; an uncirculated lot; most of the pieces bright, and many rare.

COINS OF FRANCE.

Silver.

1220 FRANCIS I.; half testoon; poor but very rare.

1221 LOUIS XIIII.; Crown, 1648; young head, laureated; rev. plain shield crowned; very fine and rare.

1222 —— Half crown, 1653; same type; fine and rare.

1223 —— Same, 1711; old head; rev. three crowns, a lily between each; extremely fine and rare.

1224 LOUIS XV.; Crown of 1759; *M. M. Stork*; nearly uncirculated; very rare.

1225 —— Same; old head (1774); *M. M. flower*; a fine crown; not equal to the last.

1226 REPUBLIC, 1851; five francs *by Oudino*; head of Ceres; rev. Liberty, Egalite, etc.; extremely fine.

Coins of Spain—Silver.

1227 REPUBLIC, 1873; three figures standing; rev. 5 FRANCS, 1873; brilliant.
1228 NAPOLEON III., 1852; 1 franc; uncirculated, scarce.
1229 —— 1860; 1 franc; uncirculated, scarce.
1230 —— 50 cent, 1860, and same 1866, with a crown on reverse, etc.; uncirculated, rare.
1231 HENRY V.; 1 franc, 1831; bust of the Pretender in military dress; uncirculated, very rare.

Copper.

1232 LIARDS and other small coppers of the kings and barons of the time of Louis XIII. and XIV. 10 pieces
1233 OBSIDIONAL; two very scarce. 3 pieces
1234 COPPERS of all sizes from Louis XV. 26 pieces
1235 JETONS; a great variety, many of them very fine, from size 14 to 20. 23 pieces
1236 BUONAPARTE, General-in-chief, etc., 1796; young bust; rev. Pallas seated; a very beautiful medalet or jeton; brass; uncirculated and bright. Size 22
1238 —— Souvenir immortal, 1840; in copper and tin, with loops varieties. 2 pieces
1239 HUNGER Jeton of 1816 and 1817; and revolutionary medalets, dollar size, brass, and brass mounted; rare and fine lot. 3 pieces
1240 NAPOLEON III., Commemorating his birth and coronation; fine brass; extremely rare. Size 22
1241 NICHOLAS Kederus Holminensis, Barclay De Tolli, and Klippes; extra lot. 5 pieces

COINS OF SPAIN.

Silver.

1242 ISABELLA II., 1859; Pillar dollar; very fine.
1243 REPUBLIC, 1870; Pillar dollar; 5 pesetas, 900 milesimas- 40 piezas en kilogramme (which is tolerably explicit); very fine, and not common.
1244 AMADEUS I.; Pillar dollar; same description as last; very fine, also scarce.

Coins of Russia—Copper. 71

1245 PESETA of Barcelona, 1812; quarter of Charles III., and base dollar of Charles IV.; of a rare type, gilt.
3 pieces

Copper.

1246 PHILIP III. and Philip IV.; uncommon; size 16.
3 pieces

1247 CHARLES II.; round and square; rare. 2 pieces

1248 CHARLES IV., and Ferdinand VII. 5 pieces

1249 BARCELONA; 4 quartos; Isabella II., and a beautiful large copper "Diez gramos," of the Rep., 1870.
4 pieces

1250 UNCLASSIFIED. 6 pieces

COINS OF RUSSIA.

Silver.

1251 ANNA; Rouble of 1731; bust of the Empress, surmounted by a small crown, legend in Russian, BY THE GRACE OF GOD EMPRESS AND AVTOCRAT OF ALL THE RVSSIAS; rev. the imperial eagle bearing a shield with the national arms; St. George and the dragon; extra broad, fine and rare.

1252 ELIZABETH I.; Rouble of 1757; same description; a fine coin, the obv. a little rubbed; scarce.

1253 NICHOLAS; Rouble of 1843; obv. the imperial eagle, with the national shield surrounded by the order, chain, and badge of the order of St. Andrew; on each wing of the eagle 3 separate shields; rev. MONEY ROVBLE in Russian characters within a wreath united by the imperial Russian crown; uncirculated; splendid, rare.

1254 ——— 25 and 20 copecs; uncirculated. 2 pieces

Copper.

1255 PETER I., the Great, 1725; voided cross, inscriptions within; rev. imperial Russian eagle; fine and rare.
Size 18

1256 PETER II., and Anna, from 1730 to 1740; fine and rare lot; average size 16.   8 pieces
1257 IVAN III., 1740 and 1744; very rare coins.   2 pieces
1258 ELIZABETH, 1741 to 1762.   17 pieces
1259 KATHARINE II., 1762 to 1796, including the large five copeck pieces.   7 pieces
1260 SIBERIA, five copecks, 1768, under Elizabeth Petrovna; arms, two foxes for supporters; fine and rare.
1261 PAUL I., 1786 to 1801; five copecks; fine; size 32.
1262 ALEXANDER I., 1801 to 1825; five and two copecks; extra fine.   3 pieces
1263 NICHOLAS I., including two toll checks, said to be rare, a fine and varied lot.   14 pieces

SILVER COINS OF AUSTRIA.

1264 RUDOLPH II., 1576 1612; uncirculated, hammered Crown of 1592, bust; rev. imperial eagle; rare.
1265 —— Same of 1600; beautiful; rare.
1266 —— Uncirculated double Crown of 1604 for the Tyrol; laureated bust in high ruff military collar and cloak; rev. arms on round shield under a crown, the shield garnished; very rare.
1267 MATTHIAS 1612 to 1619, Crown; bust of Matthias crowned; rev. arms, poor, rare.
1268 FERDINAND II., 1619–1637; Crown of 1123; bust as before; rev. the imperial eagle bearing the arms of Austria; very fine.
1269 FERDINAND III., 1637–1657; laureated bust, long hair, without the ruff, lace collar turned down; Roman habbit; rev. shield encircled by the Order Chain and Badge of the Order of the Golden Fleece; extra fine and rare crown.
1270 LEOPOLD I., 1658–1705; splendid uncirculated burnished Crown of 1691; bust laureated in rich dress and decorations; rev. like last; rare.

Silver of Various Countries.

1271 LEOPOLD I., Equally fine Crown of the next year (1692); rev. arms on the imperial eagle; has had a loop, now removed. Size 29
1272 —— Half-Crown; same type, 1703; uncirculated.
1273 CHARLES VI., 1711–1740; beautiful half-crown, 1720; rare.
1274 CHARLES VII.; never acknowledged Emperor, but sustained by Frederick the Great of Prussia; laureated bust in armor, on his neck the order-chain of the Golden Fleece; rev. the imperial eagle bearing on his breast a shield with the fir cone AVGVSTA VIN DELICORVM, 1743; nearly proof crown, rare.
1275 SMALL and generally uncirculated coins of the 3 groschen (dime) size, of all the foregoing, excepting Charles VII., with one of Charles V., which is rare, a great variety of reverses; excellent lot. 12 pieces
1276 SIMILAR lot, representing besides a great many free towns under different emperors, some VI groschen or pistareen size. 27 pieces
1277 CURIOUS and remarkable collection of early bracteates, klippes, and pennies; so far as I have examined them without duplicates, nearly all uncirculated, and covering probably five hundred years of history; such a collection as I have never before *dumped* into a catalogue in a single lot. 67 pieces
1278 GERMAN and Dutch coins; some base ½ Gulden, 2½ Gruschen, 6 krs, etc. 10 pieces

SILVER OF VARIOUS COUNTRIES.

Coins and Medals.

1279 MANSFIELD (in Prussia); crown of Peter Ernest, John Albert, John Hoyer, Bruno, Hoyer Christorf, Counts, (15)84; coat-of-arms; rev. knight and dragon; fine and rare.
1280 —— Similar of (15)91; silver crown, gilt, a different line of Counts, as Peter Ernest, Bruno, Gebhard, etc., in other respects like last; very fine and rare.

1281 SILESIA, Frederick Duke, 1623; bust; rev. coat-of-arms, crown; fine, a few scratches, rare.

1282 SAXONY (Altenburg); crown of Frederick William I., 1582; obv. figure of the Grand-Duke in mail to the hips, over his armor a fur-lined cloak, titles circumscribing the whole in a double circle; rev. picture of his brother John in the same style; the piece well set in a silver cable, loop removed; nearly uncirculated.

A similar one described by Wellenheim as very rare.

1283 —— Augsburg Confession Crown to commemorate the completion of the first century; obv. John George, Duke, in his robes, on his head a cap, sword in hand, LVTHER, AVG. EXHIBITÆ SECVLVM CONFESS JOH-GEOR, 1630, 25 Juny; rev. bust of John in the same style, TURRIS FORTISSIMA NOMEN DOMINI, JOAN-NES, 1530, 25 Juny; uncirculated burnished crown, perfectly magnificent, very rare.

1284 —— Crown of Christian, John George, and Augustus, 1598; half-length front-face figures of the three brothers; rev. coat-of-arms; very fine, nearly uncirculated.

1285 —— Duplicate; fine.

1286 OSNABURG, Sede Vacante Crown, 1698; St. Peter standing at his feet the arms of Osnaburg; rev. a church; Madai 861; very fine and rare.

1287 BAMBERG, Marquard Sebastian, Bishop 1691, Crown; a cathedral supported by two saints, shield and crown below; rev. St. Mary, CLYPEVS, etc.; Madai 779; fine crown.

1288 OLMUTZ, Charles, Duke of Lorraine, Bishop; bust with long curly hair, CAROLVS EPISCOPVS OLOMVCENSIS; rev. arms, two fierce birds supporting: DVX. LOTHAR. ET. BAR; splendid uncirculated crown, 1706; very rare.

1289 BENEDICT XIV.; Pont Max; bust; rev. the Virgin and church in the clouds, Dollar or Scudo; uncirculated and brilliant; rare.

1290 PIUS IX.; 20 Baroche; uncirculated.

Silver of Various Countries.

1291 LOMBARDY; Provisional Government, 1848; 5 size, very fine.

1292 BOHEMIA; Frederick von der Pfalz, 1619-1620; obv. bust with ducal crown under it (48); rev. arms filling the area, circumscribed by DVX. BA. MAR., MO DVX. SILE. MAR. LVSA, 1620, two Guilden, or, according to Wellenheim, Thaler; perfectly uncirculated, and although there are four in this place, pronounced in all catalogues rare.

1293 —— Duplicate; same in all respects.
1294 —— Same.
1295 —— Same.
1296 —— Gulden, (24) under bust; same Duke, also 1620; as fine as the others, rare.
1297 —— Gulden, 1620; obv. crown; rev. lion; brilliant, rare.
1298 —— Same; a duplicate; very fine.
1299 MECKLENBURG; Thaler of Christian Louis, Duke 1678; extra fine, rare.
1300 HOLSTEIN; Christian Albert, Duke 1656-1691; mailed bust, barehead; rev. coat-of-arms, ⅔ crown, 1683; extra fine, rare.
1301 SAYN-WITTGENSTEIN (in Prussia) Thaler, ⅔ (crown) of Gustavus, Count 1676; bust in Roman style, long flowing hair; rev. coat-of-arms, TANDEM, FORTVNA, OBSTETRICE; uncirculated, very rare.
1302 —— Duplicate; equally fine.
1303 BATTHYANI (in Hungary); crown of Prince Charles, 1764; bust, hair in queue; rev. splendid coat-of-arms and titles; extremely fine; very rare.
1304 BRUNSWICK; Medal Crown of 1679; obv. bust of John Frederick; rev. a palm tree springing from the summit of a rock in the sea, EX DURIS GLORIA; extra fine, rare.
1305 —— ⅛ Dollar; same type, 1673; in this, two ships in the offing; extra fine and rare.
1306 —— XII. Marien Groschen, 1670, and another same size. 2 pieces

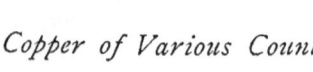

Copper of Various Countries.

Graham 1.75 1307 MEDAL, crown size; obv. St. George slaying the Dragon, S. GEORGIVS EQVITVM PATRONVS; rev. ship in a storm, IN TEMPESTATE, SECVRITAS; burnished, very fine and rare.

Sampson 1.87 1308 —— Baptism of Christ, double dollar size; inscription in Dutch; extremely fine. *Tuc* Size 34

Harriot 1.12 1309 —— Ferdinand VII. of Spain; EN PREMIO DE LA FIDELIDAD; dollar size, fine silver, cast and gilt; fine and extremely rare.

Logan .70 1310 —— Frederick William III., Prussia; Medal Thaler, 1818; fine.

do .10 1311 —— Shell of Dr. Martin Luther, only the bust and ⅓ thaler of M. Therese. 2 pieces

Stauein 2.00 1312 —— William, the present Kaiser; struck after the war 1871; bust; rev. Germania seated; very fine thaler.

Baum... .40 1313 —— Hieronymus Napoleon, King of Westphalia; ⅔ crown, 1811; has his bust; very fine and rare.

do 4.00 1314 CHOP DOLLAR of Ferdinand VII., covered with the trademarks of Chinese merchants.

Prosky .25 1315 TURKISH Quarter-Dollar; fine and two of Tunis, in all 4 pieces

Maxwell .50 1316 JAPANESE Itzbu and Quarter do. 2 pieces

Prosky 1.25 1316* —— Gold Dollar of Bechtler "27 grs."; fine.

Copper Coins and Medals.

Hastin 3.00 1317 KINGDOM of Anam, in Asia; large coin of fine yellow brass, cast in a mould, with a round hole in centre, the rim thick and flat, Oriental characters on both sides—on the principal side, twelve animals following each other in a circle around the coin; fine and rare, diameter 2 inches.

do 2.75 1318 —— Similar; animals and trees on both sides; same size, equally fine and rare.

do 2.00 1319 —— Similar; with a square hole, winged dragons instead of animals.

do 1.30 1320 —— Set of these curious coins, 3 sizes. 3 pieces

do 1.75 1321 CHINESE Coins of the same general description as last; with characters only, thick, 2½ inches broad, rare.

do .5 1322 —— Cash. 19 pieces

Copper of Various Countries. 77

1323 JAPAN Tempos; fine. 2 pieces 40 Maxwell

1324 SWEDISH Coins, series of Christina, 1632–1654, etc., and Charles XI, 1660–1697, with some later. 17 pieces 12 Pierson

1325 —— Full set of Baron Goeretz's dalers; circulated, but fair, rare. 10 pieces 8 Hall

1326 —— Plug pure copper; 1 oz. weight. 35 Haseltine

1327 SICILY, Belgium, Mecklenburg (bull's head), Cleves, Ulrecht, Zeeland, Guelders, etc., etc.; fine and rare lot coins and jetons. 30 pieces 2 do

1328 CANADA; great variety, no duplicates. 24 pieces 6 do

1328* —— Bag of old coppers. 55 pieces 2" do

1329 MEDAL of Francis I. (France); obv. laureated bust; rev. two globes, celestial and terrestrial, a crown above both VNVS NON SVFFICIT ORBIT MDXV.; extra fine bronze. Size 38 1.13 Harriot

1330 —— SECVNDA EPOCA, two hemispheres, CON LA TRIPLE GARANTIA; poor, copper. Size 36 10 Nichols

1331 —— Charles IV. and Queen *Aloisiae* of Spain, and one of Philip and Mary of England; the last cast. 2 pieces 5 do

1332 —— Æsculapius Medal, engraved on it, "J. W. J. Boscher, 1800;" brass medal cast; much older than the ins., rare. 75 Cogan

1333 —— William Beckford, Esq., 1770; his bust, three-quarter face, "The zealous advocate," etc.; extremely fine, copper. Size 28 1.00 do

1334 —— Frederick William IV. in Berlin, iron; one of Martin Luther, in tin; and Medal of the Infant Orphan Asylum at Wanstead, England, in bronze; all fine and valuable. Size 30. 3 pieces 90 Cogan

1335 MEDAL made of copper from the roof of a church in Hamburg, etc., etc., and one in copper, gilt, for presentation by the Academy of Medicine in Belgium; both very fine. Size 28. 2 pieces 25 Haseltine

1336 —— Old gothic, with loops—Henry Clay Medal, Russian, etc., etc. 12 pieces 10 Harriot

ANTIQUE COINS.

1337 FIRST brass of Hadrian, Faustina, Gordian III., and Alexander Stevens; a good lot. 4 pieces
1338 SECOND do. of Trajan, Domitian, M. Aurelius, and Johannes; fine. 5 pieces
1339 THIRD do., uncommonly fine; a very choice lot. 6 pcs
1340 SILVER of Sept, Severus, and Philip. 5 pieces
1341 JEWISH Medal, often described and engraved; head of Moses; rev. Hebrew inscription; like all others of the kind cast.
1342 GREEK, Egyptian, etc., etc., copper. 20 pieces

Silver—Various.

1343 DOLLAR of Holland (Belgic Confederation); scratches in the planchet, but uncirculated.
1344 —— 960 Rees of Brazil; uncirculated.
1345 HALF do., 400 Rees, Portugal, do.
1346 QUARTER do., 160 Rees, do.
1347 FIVE FRANCS, Lucca and Piombino; two heads; fine.
1348 —— Napoleon " Premier Consul;" good.
1348* DESM FRANC do.; uncirculated; rare.
1348** TWO FRANCS, Gioacchino Napoleon; extremely fine, *beautiful*, rare.
1349 SHILLING, Sixpence, and Threepence of George III.; uncirculated. 3 pieces
1350 THREEPENCE, Charles II.; ordinary.

Addenda to Part II.

1351 ALEXANDER III., of Scotland, A. D. 1249-1327; silver Penny; ex. fine, rare.
1352 DAVID II., Scotland, 1329-1370; Groat; crowned head in profile, sceptre; rev. long cross; fine, rare.
1353 —— Duplicate, equally fine.
1354 HENRY II., England, 1154-1189; Penny; full face and sceptre; rev. short cross; very fine.
1355 —— Duplicates. 2 pieces

English Coins. 79

1356 HENRY III., 1216-1272; bust, full face, above the head
    cross; rev. long voided cross; very fine Penny; rare.
1357 —— Duplicate.
1358 EDWARD II. and Edward III., from 1307; Penny
    crowned head, full face; rev. long cross; in each angle
    three pellets; fine.
1359 —— Another, same; equally fine.
1360 —— Others.   2 pieces
1361 HENRY VI., 1422-1461; London Groat; extra fine,
    rare.
1362 —— Calais Groat; very good.
1363 EDWARD IV., 1461-1483; London Groat; fine.
1364 —— Duplicate; very good.
1365 HENRY VII., 1483-1509; Durham Penny; the King
    seated, in his hand a crozier; struck by order of Bishop
    Sherwood; well preserved, and very rare.
1366 —— Sovereign or broad piece in gold; the King in a
    ship; rev. ornate cross, broken and joined; rare.
1367 HENRY VIII., 1509-1547; Sixpence; profile head
    crowned; rev. arms arranged on a shield; very good.
1368 —— Sixpence and threepence.   2 pieces
1369 EDWARD VI., 1547-1553; Shilling; full face; rev.
    arms, very good, scarce.
1370 MARY, 1553-1558; Groat; extremely fine, and equally
    rare; valuable.
1371 —— Duplicate; very good and rare.
1372 ELIZABETH, 1558-1603; Shilling; very fine.
1373 —— Sixpence; equally fine.
1374 —— Threepence; fair.
1375 —— Penny; fair.
1376 —— Irish Groat; fine and very rare.
1377 —— Duplicate, 3d.; poor.
1378 JAMES I., 1603-1625; Shilling; fair.
1379 —— Half-groats; fine.   3 pieces
1380 CHARLES I., 1625-1649, Oxford half-crown; feathers
    behind; rev. RELIG-PR., etc.; rubbed, but very rare.
1381 —— Half-crown; the King with drawn sword on horse-
    back; rev. arms on oval shield; better than usually
    found; but little rubbed, rare.

80   English Coins.

1382 CHARLES I. Shilling; mint mark, triangle; coined at York; very fine, scarce.
1383 —— Same; M. M. bell; ordinary, rare.
1384 —— Twopence; extra fine.
1385 CHARLES II., 1660–1685; Groat, by *Simon*; bust crowned; rev. shield on a cross; very good and rare.
1386 —— Groat and threepence; new coinage.   2 pieces
1387 JAMES II., 1685–1689; gun money—XXX d, and XII; fine.   2 pieces
1388 ANNA, 1702–1714; Edinburg half-crown; well preserved.
1389 —— Shilling; uncirculated, very rare.
1390 —— Duplicate; very good.
1391 GEORGE II., 1727–1760; Shilling and Sixpence. 2 pcs
1392 GEORGE III., 1760–1820; copper, twopence.
1393 —— A B C Medal, in tin, used in the days of our forefathers to teach the young idea how to shoot; a ribbon on it 100 years old; very fine and rare. Size 24
1394 —— Shilling; very fine (1787).
1395 VICTORIA, 1837—still reigning; War medal for India; ex. fine and rare, silver.   Size 12
1396 —— Tin medals, model coins, medals of her children, etc.; fine lot.   8 pieces
[A few silver coins, mostly German; arranged by date.]

1397 1690, Thaler of Frederick I., Prussia; poor.
1398 1705, Frederick Aug. I., Poland; base thaler, well preserved, and very rare.
1399 1740, Medal coin of Basle, in Switzerland; view of the city BASILEA, named by Julian II. (Apostate) in honor of his mother; rev. winged monster, and motto, "May God preserve us;" extra fine and rare.   Size 18
1400 1745, Splendid medal of Francis I. of Germany; rev. the Emperor and Empress (Maria Therese) in a chariot, Victory drawing the horses, three abreast; nearly proof.   Size 28
1401 1774, Silver Heller of the city of Frankfort, seat of the German diet; proof.   Size 14

Miscellaneous Silver Coins.

1792, Jubilee medal of the Count Palatine; fiftieth anniversary. Size 14
1795, ¾ crown, and 1797 crown, Denmark and Austria; both poor. 2 pieces
1816, Medal of Francis I., Emperor of Austria, with Caroline of Bavaria, their busts accolated; rev. helmeted female supported by an eagle; very fine, dollar size.
1817, Reformation Jubilee Medal, 3d centenary; inscription; extra fine, rare. Size 16
1818, Maximilian Joseph, King of Bavaria; medal crown, nearly uncirculated.

(End of coins referred to in last note.)

Miscellaneous Silver Coins.

DOLLAR of Bolivia, 1830; bust of the Liberator.
—— of Mexico, 1838; pierced.
—— of Maximilian, Emperor of Mexico, 1866; good.
—— Duplicate; more rubbed.
—— Provisional, re-struck in 1812, by the General of the Revolutionary Army.
FIVE Lire of Victor Emanuel, 1871, as King of Italy; uncirculated, rare.
DOLLAR, Episcopal of Max. Joseph of Bavaria, 1772; nearly uncirculated.
HALF Dollars of Charles IV., of Spain; pierced. 3 pcs.
QUARTER Dollars; some pierced, others much circulated. 10 pieces
20 Baiocchi, Pius IX.; fine.
SHILLINGS of Geo. III. and Victoria, (varieties). 4 pcs.
—— James I.; pierced; sixpence of Elizabeth and Geo. III.; gilt. 3 pieces
FIVE Francs of the French Republic, 1850; fine.
—— of Napoleon III., 1870; rubbed.
FRANC, 50 centimes, and 20 do. Nap. I.; very fine. 3 pieces
REALS (⅛ doll.), and others, same size. 8 pieces
HALF Real tokens, "Café Espagnol, Caraccas;" proof, and said to be extremely rare. 2 pieces

1424 SMALL Coins; average value 6 cents.   12 pieces
1425 BASE Silver Coins.   70 pieces
1426 SIAM Half Tical (30 cts); uncirculated, rare.
1427 —— Fifth do. 12 do.   do.   do.

United States Silver.

1428 DOLLAR of 1795; flowing hair; rubbed.
1429 —— 1796, Very good.
1430 —— 1798, Fair to poor.   2 pieces
1431 —— 1799, Rubbed.   do.
1432 —— 1800, Circulated, but fair.   do.
1433 —— 1803, Rubbed.
1434 —— 1850, Rubbed.
1435 —— 1865, Proof; slight scratches.
1436 —— 1867, do. do. do.
1437 —— 1871, Fine impression.
1438 —— 1873, Very fine; scarce.
1439 —— 1873, Same.   do.
1440 HALF DOLLAR, 1794: poor, scarce.
1441 —— 1803; good example, but rubbed.
1442 —— 1806;   "   "   "
1443 —— 1807; rubbed.
1444 —— 1808; poor.
1445 —— 1810;   "
1446 —— 1811;   "
1447 —— 1818;   "
1448 —— 1819;   "
1449 —— 1828; pierced.
1450 —— 1830; very good.
1451 —— 1831; fair, rubbed.
1452 —— 1832; good.
1453 —— 1833;   "
1454 —— 1836 & '7; poor.   2 pieces
1455 —— 1851;   "
1456 —— 1855;   "
1457 —— 1859; fine.
1458 —— 1860; very good.
1459 —— 1861;   "

Colonial and State Coppers, Cents, etc. 83

1460 HALF DOLLAR, 1863; very good.
1461 ——— 1864; "
1462 ——— 1865; poor.
1463 ——— 1866; fine.
1464 ——— 1867; very fine.
1465 ——— 1869; "
1466 ——— 1870; one E B FARR; card.   2 pieces
1467 ——— 1871; one, fine.   2 "
1468 ——— 1874; very fine.
1469 QUARTER DOLLARS; 1807, '15, '18, '20, '21, '25, '28, etc.; poor lot.   12 pieces
1470 ——— 1862; very fine.
1471 DIMES ranging between 1805 & '74; generally poor.   25 pieces
1472 HALF DIME of 1795; fine, rare.
1473 ——— Some scarce dates poor, common dates fine.   30 pieces
1474 THREE CENTS; ordinary.   11 pieces
1475 PINE TREE SHILLING; poor, rare.
1476 CHALMER's Annapolis; poor, rare.

COLONIAL & STATE COPPERS, CENTS, &c.

1477 MASSACHUSETTS CENTS, 1787 & 1788; much circulated.   3 pieces
1478 ——— 1788; very fair.
1479 NOVA CONSTELLATIO; 3 varieties; fair to poor.   7 pieces
1480 NOVA CAESAREA; different, fair.   4 pieces
1481 VERMONTENSIUM, and another Vermont, with the head and title of George III. Rex. in fair condition, and rare, the first poor.   2 pieces
1482 CONNECTICUT CENTS; variety, ordinary.   5 pieces
1483 FRANKLIN CENTS; poor.   7 "
1484 CENTS (U. S.); from the first year, 1793, '94, '95, '96, '97, '98, no '99, no 1804, but nearly a full set to 1874, including many 2 cents; nearly all poor.   96 pieces
1485 HALF-CENTS; indifferent.   36 "

84 *Miscellaneous.*

1486 NICKEL 5 cents; fine, (1870–74). 5 pieces
1487 —— 3 cents. 3
1488 PATTERN CENT of 1854; head without ins.; fine.
1489 —— Cent of 1855; flying eagle; fine.
1490 STORE CARDS and Copperheads. 10 pieces
1491 POLITICAL MEDALETS; Jackson, Clay, Van Buren, Harrison, Fremont, Cass, and Lincoln. 9 pieces
1492 WASHINGTON; copy of the half dollar of 1792; splendid proof, copper.
1493 —— Two medalets, Baltimore Monument and Coin Dealers' Card; poor. 2 pieces
1494 CONTINENTAL Currency; fine proof copy in bronze.
1495 CENTENNIAL Medal, 1776–1876, IN MEMORIAL; fine proof, tin. Size 27
1496 CONFEDERATE Cent, 1861, head of Liberty in Phrygian cap, CONFEDERATE STATES of AMERICA; rev. 1 CENT within a wreath of corn, wheat, etc; copper, fine proof; excessively rare.

By Lovett, of Philadelphia, a few copies struck, and dies destroyed.

MISCELLANEOUS.

1497 CARRARA Medal, Jacobus Grandis, 1323; bust in pointed hood; rev. arms; thick bronze. Size 44
1498 —— Marsilius Major De Carraria, 1324; bust in a sort of cowl, with vest buttoned on the shoulder; rev. same as last. Same size

These fine and rare bronzes were executed by one of the great artists of the 15th century, who revived in Italy the forgotten art of the medallests. Vittor Pisano, Matteo d'Pasté, and others, founded a school, where they modelled profile heads of illustrious men and women, adorning the reverses with designs of admirable workmanship in relief. The Carrara medals seldom appear in European, and until quite recently, never in American catalogues.

1499 Box OF siftings from the excavations recently made by the American Holy Land Exploring Expedition near the outer wall of the old temple at Jerusalem; a hundred or more pieces of copper, with impressions of dies

Miscellaneous. 85

1500 Box of SIFTINGS, etc. ; Similar.
1501 —— Same.
1502 TESSERAE, or little tokens in lead, from excavations at Pompeii ; very perfect. 10 pieces
1503 Box of modern base coins. 16 "
1504 Box of medals of royal children, with the Prince Consort and Queen—minute ; very fine. 8 pieces
1505 JAPANESE (tempo), Chinese (cash), Native Indian, and East India Co.'s coins. 21 pieces
1506 BARBADOES, Liberia, Ceylon, and Demarara copper coins, several uncommon. 10 pieces
1507 WOOD's pennies and half-pennies, Gun money, "God preserve London," and others; English. 10 pieces
1508 SPANISH pattern coins in brass, being impressions from genuine dies, marked by a bar to prevent imposition, etc. ; together with several fine and rare French tokens and pieces of necessity and convenience ; several valuable coins in the lot. 12 pieces
1509 COPY in tin of Cromwell half-crown, and galvanized pennies resembling silver. 10 pieces
1510 FRENCH medalets: Souvenir Immortel, etc., Napoleon I. and II., and Revolution of 1848. 3 pieces
1511 SCOTCH coins, medalets, and miscellaneous. 20 "
1512 MEDALS in copper, brass, and tin ; poor, but original and very rare ; Charles I., Anne, and George III. on his death. Av. size, 30. 4 pieces
1513 —— Similar, including the Lafayette medal ; some without reverses, many of them poor. 12 pieces
1514 COPPER coins, penny size. 50 "
1515 —— Two and one-penny size. 30 "
1516 Box of old American cents. 340 "
1517 —— of old coppers, half-penny size. 735 "
1518 —— with several rare pieces, e.g. the "Floreat Rex," Irish farthing, mule of the "Talbot, Allum and Lee," etc., etc. 100 pieces

Miscellaneous.

A few choice Medals and Coins, selected.

1519 Dr. Martin Luther, fine bust, inscription; rev. ZUR GEDAECHTNISSFEIER DES 18 FEB., 1846, IN WITTENBERG; splendid proof in bronze by *Looz;* rare. Size 28

1520 Medal; angel measuring the world, "Unite des Mesures;" rev. Genius standing with a measuring-rod, "Ce tous les temps a tous les Peuples," the base marked and graduated "Cinq Centimetre" (to commemorate the National Convention, etc.); bronze, proof. Size 44

1521 Charles X., King of France; fine medal by *Rogat,* bust; rev. SACRE A REIMS, (in case); proof, bronze. Size 25

1522 Napoleon III., on his election, 1852; splendid proof by *Dantzell,* copper. Size 18

1523 —— with Eugenie; marriage medal, their heads; brass, gilt, proof. Size 22

1524 Monneron's Cinq Sols (uncirculated), "10-cent" colonial of L. Philippe, Napoleon III. 10-centimes; bright, and others of equally good quality; a fine lot of French coins and medalets. 10 pieces

1525 Medalets, Meraux, and Jetons of France; fine. 10 pieces

1526 Money Weights; Italy, France, and Spain. 7 "

1527 Kamehameha of Hawaii, 10 Lepta of Greece, dos quartos of Gibraltar, Wood's half-penny, Belgian, etc., etc.; selected coins, all *fine.* 15 pieces

1528 Base silver coins of the Porte; many varieties of larger size, and fine; one pierced. 8 pieces

1529 Fine do., half-dime size; uncirculated. 8 "

1530 —— do., of the value of a rupee, together with a rupee of India, struck by the English E. I. Co. 2 pieces

1531 Dollar of Peru, 1865 (very fine), and one of Ferd. VII. of Spain, struck in Mexico. 2 pieces

1532 Pius IX. and Napoleon III.; 20 baiocchis of the former and 1 franc of the latter; brilliant. 2 pieces

Miscellaneous Coins, Medals, and Tokens.   87

1533 VICTOR EMANUEL, William II. of the Netherlands, Francis Joseph of Austria, etc., etc.; average ½ franc.
10 pieces

1534 FLORIN of Victoria (wanting D. G. to title, and rare), with U. S. quarter-dollar, English shilling, etc.
4 pieces

1535 GOLD dollar (1/16 doubloon), Charles III., Spain.

MISCELLANEOUS COINS, MEDALS, & TOKENS.

1536 COLONIAL and State cents: Nova Cæsarea, Auctori Connec, Massachusetts, Franklin cent, and Washington cent (Unity States); poor.   20 pieces

1537 CENTS (U. S.), early dates, and poor, but with fair 1794, '95, and '97 (Feuchtwanger in the lot).   22 pieces

1538 HALF-CENTS and Shinplasters; ordinary.   20 pieces

1539 POLITICAL Medalets, Store Cards, 5 cent postage stamp mounted, etc., etc.; all fine.   20 pieces

1540 COPPERHEADS; bright and uncirculated.   100 pieces

1541 TIN Medals, Great Eastern, French Rev. '48, visit of Victoria to France, Empress Eugenie and McClellan; from size 18 to 26, fine.   5 pieces

1542 FORT SUMTER Medal.   Size 42

1543 BASE silver and counterfeit coins.   34 pieces

1544 FINE do small coins, average value, 5 cents.   6 pieces

1545 ANTIQUE, large and small brass.   8 pieces

1546 JAPANNED tin cash-box with tray and till, and within 300 coins and medals, sold together.

1547 POLITICAL Medals, Grant and Sherman, tin and copper; size 20.   2 pieces

1547* —— Winfield Scott; rev. wreath; copper, proof.
Size 28

1548 QUARTER Dollars; gold, California.   2 pieces

1549 SILVER Ducat, dime size; rare.

1550 SILVER coins from penny to franc size.   9 pieces

1551 GEORGE III. and Charlotte medalet, with their busts, together with old Crusader's coin and bracteate; silver.   3 pieces

Fine Silver Coins and Medals.

1552 UNITED STATES Cents; old dates, none fine, but all too good to throw away. 25 pieces

1553 PRUSSIAN War Medal; 1866; the device within cross and crown, Monneron's Cinq Sols. Temperance Medal, etc.; copper and tin. 5 pieces

1554 SILVER of Pius IX., 20 Baiocchi and Turkish Quarter Dollar; fine silver, very fine. 2 pieces

1555 ANTIQUE of Augustus, Agrippa, Antonia, etc. 6 pieces

1556 —— Constantine and his Sons. 15 pieces

1557 OLD COLONIAL and other American coppers, etc., all very poor. 27 pieces

Fine Silver Coins and Medals.

1558 JOHN HUSS, Memorial Dollar; obv. bust; rev. his martyrdom; to commemorate his being burnt as a Reformer in 1415; of the few sold, one of the best, very rare.

1559 RIX Dollar, 1618; Denmark the first of the 30 years' war; the King crowned; rev. a large crown; extra fine and rare.

1560 CROWN; Denmark during the 30 years' war; thick, size 14, a great rarity, in good preservation.

1561 —— 1649; Brunswick at the close of the 30 years' war; Army of Brunswick and Luneburg; rev. wild man standing; rare.

1562 MANSFIELD; Third Crown of John George, Count, 1671; coat-of-arms; rev. knight transfixing a monster; fine and rare.

1563 BRUNSWICK; Guilder of the Hartz, 1701; wild man standing (XXIIII Marien Grosch); very fine, scarce.

1564 SHOLBERG; Guilder of 1704; rev. stag.

1565 BRUNSWICK; Guilder of 1711, except date, same as 1563; equally fine.

1566 MEDAL to Commemorate a Confederation in 1791; bust of Leopold II.; rev. SIC FOEDERA JVNGVNT; extra fine, dollar size, rare.

1567 RELIGIOUS Medal (Communion); bust of the Saviour; rev. interior of a church; extra fine, dollar size.

Antiquities.

Dr. Martin Luther, Reformation Medal to commemorate the third centenary festival, Oct., 1817; extremely fine, rare. Size 20

New York State Mexican War Medal given to the Volunteers; fine (over three dollars value in silver).

Antique Coins.

Ptolemy Soter; diademed head; rev. eagle on a thunderbolt; *extremely fine* tetradrachm; rare.

Athens; head of M nerva; rev. owl; early form of the tetradrachm; good example.

Greek Imperial; obv. head of Nero; rev. head of Jupiter Serapis; base silver tetradrachm.

Hadrian; denarius, head; rev. heap of arms; good.

Severus, Gordian III., etc., denarii. 4 pieces

Greek Copper of the 3d size; Locris, Macedon, and Sicyon. 3 pieces

First brass of Philip (Roman Emperor); patinated and fine.

PART III.

ANTIQUITIES.

Egyptian Bronzes (from Thebes.)

Eye from a mummy case, the natural size; the socket bronze, with opaque glass ball; imperfect, yet striking example of Outa (the mystic eye).

Tweezers, simple ornamentation; very fine and entirely perfect, length 3 inches.

Lachrymatory, with two little rings to admit a string or *bail*, length about 3 inches.

(Very rare in bronze; perhaps, as Shaw suspects, used for some other purpose.)

Vase, solid. anciently used as a symbol or ornament, diota pattern (two ears); extremely interesting and fine, length 3 inches.

90   Objects in Baked Earth, Glass, Leather, etc.

1581 OSIRIS with *tululus*, *flagellum* and *hook* in complete preservation; length, 3 inches.

    A careful examination of this fine little antique will reveal the mask in front of the *tutulus*—high winged cap.

1582 OSIRIS, represented as before; on this, however, the ornament on the *tutulus* is a hawk's beak and the leaf of some sacred plant (lotus ?), a more elaborate and important image; every part perfect, height 9 inches.

1583 —— The same deity with the hawk's head surmounted by a modius and bottle; the hands which are raised have held something now lost; it is suggested a branch of palm, feather, or some other symbolic object common to this representative of the great god of the world—the sun; the figure and all its parts with the exception noticed absolutely perfect; very rare and valuable, height 6 inches.

1584 ANUBIS, dog-headed god, on pedestal, broken; height 4 inches.

1585 ISIS, Consort of Osiris; a most beautiful and remarkable image of the horned Isis, or moon, in a sitting posture, the figure about 9 inches in height, on a pedestal retaining its peg and covered with hieroglyphics on four sides—not to be surpassed.

OBJECTS IN BAKED EARTH, GLASS, LEATHER, ETC.

(All obtained in Egypt in 1858.)

1586 ISIS (averrunca); green earthen covered with hieroglyphics: the goddess holding the hieralpha (sacred A.), net and hook, her head covered with the veil; a beautiful and perfect example, the characters not painted on the surface, but stamped into the soft paste before baking; height 10 inches.

1587 ISIS (Mother of the World) seated with Horus in her lap, on her head a throne, same material as last; a miniature figure about 2 inches high; perfect and beautiful, very rare.

Objects in Baked Earth, Glass, Leather, etc. 91

1588 ANUBIS, walking; a similar miniature figure, broken and mended; very fine.

1589 FLAT figures sewn into the wrappings of mummies, a group as originally (and frequently) found, supposed to represent the four seasons of the year; head of an eagle, jackal, lion, and old man—two blue and two drab color; 4 pieces.

(Same material and size.)

1590 NECKLACE made of hundreds of ivory rings graduated in size, so that the string looks like the asp, in the centre of the necklace two real jasper beads; length 22 inches:

1591 —— Made of glass and baked earth, beads, bugles, and charms; 35 pieces, some gilt, characteristic and valuable, sold as one lot.

1592 —— Made of colored bugles and beads, four strings and tassel; very fine.

1593 —— Similar to last, with a scarab hung as a pendant, the scarab representing a real mummied *beetle*, the swathings still remaining; extremely rare and valuable.

1594 MOSAICS and CHARM from an old temple in Upper Egypt, extra fine. 3 pieces

1595 SCARABŒUS, Baked Earth, half inch diameter.

1596 CHARMS; one, a head carved in serpentine, apparently not Egyptian work, but antique; fine lot. 6 pieces

1597 —— Similar lot, many pieces; the Eye of Horus; pieces of ivory, etc., etc.; as a lot.

1598 LAMP; Terra-Cotta, with handsome ornaments, perfect and very pretty.

1599 VASE; same material, very small.

1600 EMBOSSED Leather, fine specimens. 2 pieces

1601 PAPYRUS, characteristic and beautiful specimen, with writing in the three forms, Hieratic, Enchorial and Demotic. 15 pieces

1602 —— Same. 18 do.

1603 —— Same. 18 do.

1604 BREAD FRUIT (product of the palm-tree), found in a mummy case.

1605 PETRIFIED WOOD, bitumen and terra cotta. 4 pieces

1606 JAR for unguent, steatite, supposed to have contained paint for the eye-brows.
1607 SILVER, copper, and ivory finger rings.   3 pieces
The first Arabic.
1608 ALABASTRON; Vase for ointment or perfumes, fully described by Visconti; very rare; height 4 inches.
1609 TURQUOISE, a parcel from Egypt.
1610 ROBE OF JUSTIFICATION, supposed to be worn in the trial after death; a fine example of the linen of Ancient Egypt, in perfect preservation, about seventeen feet long by six feet wide; very rare and valuable.

ENGRAVED GEMS.

Antique Intagli.

1611 Two laureated Heads, one on the other (accolated), dark cornelian; valuable; $\frac{3}{4}$ inch.
1612 HEAD of a Satyr, clove-brown, agate, with lower stratum inclining to pink; very fine, a real gem; $\frac{3}{4}$ inch.
1613 HEAD of Minerva, in helmet; fine work, on light sardonyx; $\frac{3}{4}$ inch.
1614 HEAD of Vesta, veiled; white chalcedony; very fine and desirable; $\frac{1}{2}$ inch.
1615 SATYR milking a goat (capri-mulgus), on honey yellow sard, very fine and rare; $\frac{1}{2}$ inch.
1616 HEAD of Aurora, radiated; on a translucent stone of three colors, fine; $\frac{7}{8}$ inch.
1617 BUST in the Roman habit, a well-cut stone in fine preservation; cornelian; 1 inch.
1618 FEMALE head, Roman; very fine, nearly round; yellow cornelian; $\frac{1}{2}$ inch.
1619 YOUNG male head, light agate, cinque cento; $\frac{3}{4}$ inch.
1620 SCORPION, on blood stone, antique octagon; very fine; $\frac{5}{8}$ inch.
1621 ROMAN Youth in the toga virilis, on white chalcedony; rare; $\frac{1}{4}$ inch.
1622 BOWL on dolphin's tail, on the bowl two doves; red jasper; $\frac{1}{4}$ inch.

Engraved Gems.   93

Modern Intagli.

1623 YOUNG male bust, deep cut, and fine light red sard; 1¼ inch.
1624 HEAD of Socrates, chalcedony; ex. fine; ¾ inch.
1625 FINE oval sard, with three laureated heads accolated; a stone of excellent quality; 1 inch.
1626 NEPTUNE, standing on a shell, around him waves; deep red sard; 1 inch.
1627 BUST OF SHAKESPERE, pale sard; fine; ⅞ inch.
1628 —— Another red cornelian; ⅞ inch.
1629 BUST OF MILTON; cornelian; very fine; ⅞ inch.
1630 BUST, on square chalcedony; ⅝ inch.
1631 YOUNG HERCULES; sard; fine; ½ inch.
1632 HYMEN with torch; white agate; old polished intaglio; fine; 1¼ inch.
1633 FAME, full length figure, chalcedony, fine stone; 1 inch.
1634 LAUREATED Head in the Roman style; cornelian; 1 inch.
1635 CORNELIAN seal stones; fine heads, laureated and filleted; fine color and work.   2 pieces
1636 CLEOPATRA; the asp on her breast, and two other little gems; sard and onyx.   3 pieces
1637 OLD Roman head, clear colorless, chalcedony; fine; ⅝ in.
1638 PAIR of red cornelians; fine heads.   2 pieces
1639 PAIR, Head of Shakespeare and Companion; fine oval sards; ⅞ inch.   2 pieces
1640 CICERO and EPICURUS; two fine heads, old and excellent work; ½ inch.   2 pieces
1641 FULL length figure of Hope, and Bust of William Shakespeare, fine little stones.   2 pieces
1642 SHAKESPEARE, small ring stone, extra fine.
1643 —— and other heads; fine lot; ⅝ inch.   3 pieces
1644 FINE Seal Stones, suitable for mounting; sard of different shades; large size.   2 pieces
1645 HEADS of Socrates and Mars; old and fine stones, matched; ½ inch.   2 pieces
1646 ANOTHER matched pair, Shakespeare and Companion; ⅝ inch.   2 pieces

Miscellaneous.

1647 VARIETY of intagli, suitable for a collection; a fine lot. 7 pieces

1648 CORNELIANS with busts; the same with burning heart, and one with crescent and seven stars; a fine lot of small stones. 5 pieces

Miscellaneous.

1649 ANTIQUE intagli; Jupiter seated, in one hand a head with rays, and mate, an eagle standing on a cornucopia; dark red cornelian, ⅝ inch. 2 pieces

1650 —— Small thick stones of various kinds, all antique; the subjects as varied as the stones, Eq., Lion, vase, head in a mask, etc., from ¼ to ⅜ inch. 5 pieces

1651 —— Thinner stones, all Cornelians, a very pretty lot, same size. 5 pieces

1652 MODERN Crystal intagli for buttons; horseman leaping a bar, and dog's head, round, ⅜ inch. 2 pieces

1653 SEAL; Head of Sir Walter Raleigh, three-quarter face; in paste; gold or gilt mounting.

1654 RING, antique jasper; gold or gilt mounting.

1655 —— Tortoise Shell; coral cameo; subject laughing mask; work very old.

1656 PIN, Onyx Cameo, heavy 18k. gold mounting; done in Rome; very fine and valuable.

1657 —— Enamel'd gold and pearls; fine antique agate cameo stone; ex. fine.

1658 MATCHED pair Cornelians, pure color, suitable for sleeve buttons; modern; ⅜ inch. 2 pieces

1659 —— Onyx cameo heads. 2 pieces

1660 —— Onyx and Sadonyx stones. 2 pieces

1661 TOPAZ, brown and yellow, with letters and crest. 2 pcs

1662 CAMEI; Head of Diana (Sardonyx), and raven (pale onyx); ⅜ inch. 2 pieces

1663 AGATE, yellow and red cornelian, and sardonyx seal stones. 4 pieces

Bric-a-Brac. 95

1664 SARDONYX Camei; female heads. 2 pieces
1665 LAVA do. Diana.
1666 —— do. Madonna.
1667 —— do. Van Dyck.
1668 —— do. (a set) Cupid and Eagle; allo relievo.
3 pieces
1669 ANTIQUE Ring, mounting (modern), 14k. gold; subject Cupid, fine.
1670 CRYSTAL ball, diameter 2 inches; very fine and valuable, rare.

BRIC-A-BRAC.

1671 SAUCER for jewels; porphyry.
1672 SILVER telescopic drinking cup, coin standard, inside gilt; in case; fine and valuable.
1673 —— Tobacco box, bivalve, and genuine repousse; fine.
1674 NAUTICAL Instrument; antique, in case; very curious and rare.
1675 CAMP Clock, runs 24 hours, strikes the hours and indicates the time by touching a spring; has also an alarm attachment; was used by a British officer in the Peninsular war, and purchased of him by present owner; in handsome leather case; valuable.
1676 WINE Coolers, once the property of Sir John Harvey, who was the General opposed to Gen. Scott in the war of 1812–1815. They bear the crest of Sir John, from whom they were purchased direct in 1837; heavy silver-plated copper. 2 pieces
1677 MEDIEVAL Plaque; religious subject, figures in relief; copper gilt; 4 inch.
1678 PLAQUE; head in alto-relievo; bronze.
1679 —— Head of Bacchus; fine.
1680 —— Laureated head and trophy; bronze. 2 pieces
1681 HEAD of a Turk, a handle; fine.
1682 CHINESE Vases, old porcelain, the form cylindrical, with ornaments in relief, the colors green and red; height 15 inches. 2 pieces
1683 —— Group carved in steatite; grotesque.

1684 SNAIL in its shell; serpentine.
1685 BISQUE group, exquisitely decorated, "leap frog;" broken and mended.
1686 TERRA Cotta Bacchic group, antique, from Pompeii.
1687 ANTIQUE Knife, called Cecespeta, from Pompeii.
1688 BRONZE Figures; artistic. 2 pieces
1689 ORMULU Clock.
1690 CLOCK, bronze.
1691 PLATE, (Holland).
1692 PLAQUE, rennaissance.
1693 CARD Receiver, silver stand.
1694 CHINESE Figure.
1695 CANDLESTICK, marble.
1696 BRONZE Waiter.
1697 ELECTROTYPES. 2 pieces
1698 —— Assorted. 8 do.
1699 BACCHANALS. 4 do.
1700 ASH Tray.
1701 MEDAL.
1702 DOG'S Head, painted in oil on a smooth pebble; diameter 2½ inches.
1703 ENAMEL Paintings, Swiss scenery; small ovals. 5 pieces
1704 —— A Series do. 3 do.
1705 PAINTING on Ivory, Madonna, dolorosa; 2¼x3 inches.
1706 —— Same; Vestal Virgin; very fine; square 4¼x6 in.
1707 —— on kid, exquisitely done; Pompeian designs in Medallion.
1708 EMBROIDERY on Silk, fifteenth century; Christ on the Cross with angels ministering to him.
1709 STEREOSCOPIC Views in Egypt. 12 pieces
1710 —— Miscellaneous. 22 do.
1711 CASE of Medals, by *Andrieu;* electrotype copies of the series, viz.: Napoleon I.; the same, with Josephine; Napoleon as first Consul; siege of the Bastile, etc., etc. imperial fol., morocco, gilt.

INDIAN IMPLEMENTS, Etc.

1712 FLINT Arrow Heads ploughed up on the farm of Gen. James Wadsworth, the battle-ground where Sullivan fought the Indians in 1789.   6 pieces
1713 —— Others, larger size.   6 do.
1714 FLINT Knife, used as a *skinner*.
1715 —— Arrow Heads in case.   3 do.
1716 MODOC War Club, large and fine, rare.
1717 FLUTED Bow, length 4 feet, very fine.
1718 Bow, covered with raw hide, broken; rare.
1719 ARROWS with obsidian and iron points and feathers.   6 pieces
1720 —— Some with iron and feathers.   10 do.
1721 SNOW Shoes, large pair.
1722 Box of Beads from an Indian grave.
1723 POTTERY from an Indian mound.   4 pieces
1724 STONE Axe, remarkable form, (made to receive a wedge to tighten the handle).

> The following, from the collection of F. S. Perkins, Esq., of Burlington, Wis., are excessively rare, as are all implements in copper, dating from the era of the "Mound Builders." They are handsomely forged from virgin (unsmelted) copper, measuring from three to four inches in length. The name of the finder is attached to each, and Mr. Perkins has kindly offered to furnish the purchaser, on application to him at his address, with all desired information on the subject.

1725 SPEAR-HEAD, with voided shank to receive the handle; Owen Hearne; 3½ inches.
1726 —— Nearly a duplicate.
1727 —— Same, F. B. Dreyer; 4 inches.

MINERALS.

1728 ACADIOLITE, Partridge Island, N. S.; ex. fine specimen.
1729 STILBITE, Cape Split, N. S.; large and fine.   2 pieces
1730 —— from Partridge Island, do. do.   2 do.
1731 NATROLITE, N. S.; large and ex. fine.
1732 KYANITE, Windham, Me.

1733 ACADIOLITE, Partridge Island; large and fine.
1734 STAURODIDE, Windham, Me.; very fine. *Nelse* 2 pieces
1735 EPIDOTE, Steuben, Me.; ex. fine.
1736 AMETHYST, Blomidon, N. S.
1737 AGATE, Cape Split.
1738 LEPIDOLITE and Green Tourmaline from Paris, Me.; very fine and rare.
1739 ANALCITE, Cape Split, N. S. 2 pieces
1740 SERPENTINE, Newbury, Mass.
1741 GALENITE and Zinc Blende, Shelburne, N. H.
1742 STILBITE, Cape Split, N. S.; fine. 2 pieces
1743 ALBITE, Paris, Me.
1744 ACADIOLITE, Two Islands, N. S.; large and fine.
1745 Box of Minerals from the foregoing localities; same and other varieties.
1746 CRYSTALIZED Quartz, Mount Holy Cross.
1747 GOLD Quartz and Pyrites, Gilpin Co., Colorado.
1748 BRECCIA Marble, Boulder Co., do.
1749 SMOKY Quartz and Felaspar, Pikes Peak.
1750 ACTINOLITE, Bergen, Colorado.
1751 Moss Agate, Montana.
1752 ORE from Bonrrough's Mine, Nevada.
1753 CARBONATE of Iron, gold quartz and pyrites from California Lode, Gilpin Co., Cal.
1754 QUARTZ Crystal, Bear Creek, Cal.
1755 SPECIMEN from Forrest Rock, Georgetown, Col.
1756 PETRIFIED Moss Rock, South Park, Col.
1757 WOOD Jasper, Denver, Col.
1758 BERYL.
1759 SULPHATE of Copper, Col.
1760 FOLIATED Gypsum, Bear Creek, Col.
1761 QUARTZ Crystal; very large specimen.
1762 CHALCEDONY and Petrified Wood, Green Mountain, Cal.
1763 GALENA in Crystals, Galena, Ill.
1764 PIPE-STONE Pyrites.
1765 SPHERIOLITE Iron, El Paso Co., Col.
1766 GIBRALTAR Stone, Idaho.
1767 NAIL Head Spar, Cal.
1768 WOOD, Sardonyx, do.

Minerals.

1769 PEACOCK Gold, Gregory Mine, Cal.
1770 CALC Spar, Beaver Co., Col.
1771 CRYSTALIZED Palm-wood, South Park, Col.
1772 GYPSUM, Bear Creek, Col.
1773 PETRIFIED Cedar, South Park, Col.
1774 SULPHATE of Iron and Zinc, do.
1775 SLIKINSIDE, Seaton lode, Idaho.
1776 PETRIFIED Magnolia Wood.
1777 ROSE Quartz, Bergen, Col.
1778 LIGNITE, Cal.
1779 SILVER Ore; Spanish bar lode, Col.
1780 GOLD bearing Quartz and Pyrites, "
1781 ASPHALTUM; Turkey Creek, "
1782 GOLD Ore; Central City, "
1783 Native Alum; Turkey Creek, "
1784 SMOKY Quartz and Feld-Spar, "
1785 PUDDING Stone; El Paso Co., "
1786 GOLD Quartz Crystalized; "
1787 CHALCEDONY; South Park, "
1788 Specimen from Wood lode, Gilpin, Cal.
1789 FOLIATED Gypsum; Bear Creek.
1790 WOOD Agate; Denver Plain, Col.
1791 DRUSY Quartz; Mount of Holy Cross, Col.
1792 BARYTA; Rollin Co. "
1793 CONE Rock; Pike's Peak, "
1794 NAIL Head Spar, "
1795 GOLD Ore; Leavitt Lode, Central City, "
1796 ARROGONITE; Park Co. "
1797 CLOUDY Alabaster; Boar Creek, "
1798 BARYTA, "
1799 CUBE Calc. Spar, "
1800 CUBE Pyrites and Gold Quartz; Wyoming lode, Col.

1801 OLD Book; " Trajan's Column."
1802 " NEW YORK Water Works; " bill for eight shillings, August, 1775.
1803 —— Same for four shillings.

1804 ULSTER Co. Gazette, Jany. 4, 1800.
1805 A COLLECTION of Foreign Coins, silver and copper, many hundreds; some in wrappers with description; sold as one lot.
1806 POSTAGE STAMPS; a book nearly full, containing many of great rarity; a valuable collection as will be seen upon examination; offered here without any attempt at description; cost the owner $400.
1807 WAMPUM; a string of mixed white and black beads, made from the *Ronoake* shells; fine and valuable; length about 18 inches.
1808 BADGES, Old Newspapers, etc.; sold as one lot.
1809 COIN Cabinet; mahogany case, brass trimmings.

www.ingramcontent.com/pod-product-compliance
Lightning Source LLC
Chambersburg PA
CBHW022147160426
43197CB00009B/1467